CALIFORNIA GHOST TOWN TRAILS

by
Mickey Broman

1985 Revision by
Russ Leadabrand

Gem Guides Book Co.
315 CLOVERLEAF DR., SUITE F
BALDWIN PARK, CA 91706

A Note from the Publisher

There are many locations described in this book, and to the best of our knowledge, those to which directions are given were open to visitation at the time of publication. However, land status is changing rapidly in California.

Old mining claims are being reactivated, private properties are changing hands, some lands controlled by governments are being put under new regulations. Therefore, the inclusion of any location in this book does not guarantee that it will continue to be accessible. Watch for posting and never enter private property without permission. If there is mining equipment and/or private buildings in the area, please stay away from them

For your own safety, stay away from mine shafts. Abandoned shafts, in particular, are dangerous; ladders and timbers are often rotten and air may be bad.

Some of the locations are in remote desert regions, and a few common-sense precautions are in order. Many of these regions are best visited in the fall, winter or spring because summer temperatures can be extremely high. If you have never been into the back country of the desert, it is best to first go in with someone who is familiar with it. For remote areas we advise traveling in more than one vehicle; if one breaks down, you have a means of getting out. Take plenty of water, some cans of food and matches, just in case. Be sure that you have a good spare tire. Take along a shovel for digging out, should you get stuck in the sand. A first-aid kit is always advisable, no matter where you travel.

Wherever you go, be sure to check road and weather conditions. Back country roads can change due to natural causes, such as floods; discontinuance of maintenance; etc.

The "bottom line" is that traveling in remote areas can be quite safe — safer than city streets and freeways — but precautions must be taken against hazards, both man-made and natural. With reasonable safety measures, the ghost town explorer is on the way to a lot of enjoyment and relaxation on these journeys into our fascinating heritage.

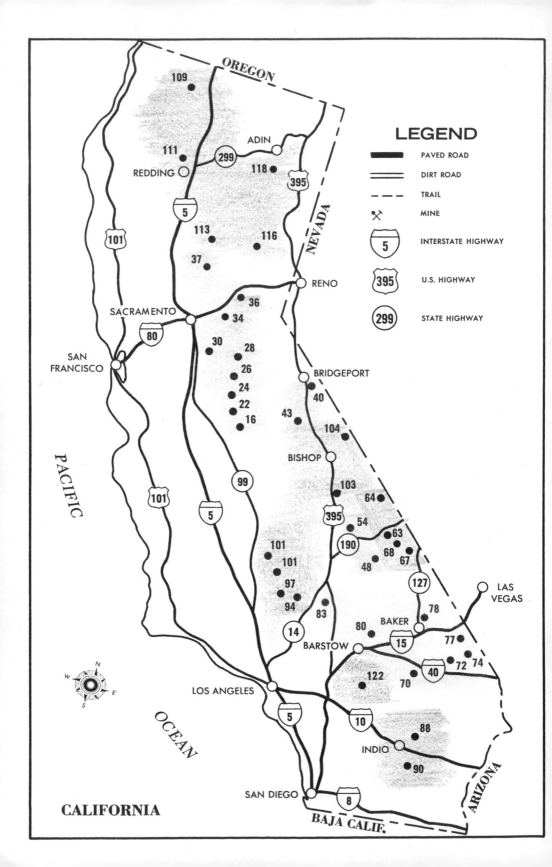

Table of Contents

Introduction

Welcome to the strange, high drama, heart break and quick fortune world of the California ghost towns. Most of them were once mining camps — dream cities. Places where fortunes could be made, but more than likely would never be made. Places where men and women from all over the world came to play out that wonderful sudden game of chance where the few lucky ones take something — almost for nothing — from Mother Earth. The quickest and easiest way that there ever was to make a fortune.

But, the odds are always quirky. True, many did become suddenly rich in these yesterday camps. However, there was always the other side of the coin.

Sometimes the shocker on that other side was that a fortune earned so quickly and easily was lost to someone else just as quickly and easily. There are those who say that on one of His less busy days God did only this: He created mining and He created, as a Godly balance, gambling.

Sometimes the other side of the coin was pure heartbreak. The Spanish had a name for it: *borrasca*, the dry hole.

At times the disappoint came in the fact that no matter how large the fortune, it was never big enough to divide up with the number of people involved in finding it.

Some of the happiest inhabitants of California's yesteryear camps were not those who found the gold. A truly happy individual was the man who found a fair meadow in which to build a home for himself and his family, and his children's family — or the person who opened a store to sell canned beans and peaches, square nails and coal oil, candles and axes, rope and work gloves. Some of the wealthiest residents of those campus were not those who grubbed and found the gold, but those who built the toll paths, then the toll roads and toll bridges, and finally the railroads, taking the miners in and the money out.

Not all of the California ghost towns were gold or silver camps. Some were logging camps, some gave up borax, others gave up nothing.

And, now a warning. Unless your jib is of a different cut than most,

6

you will be somehow ensnared by what you learn of ghost towns, particularly if it is all new to you.

You will find that reading about one camp will lead to reading about its neighbor, that going to see one ghost town will cause you to want to go and see its neighbor. You will discover that to read about and to go to look for that handful of "vanished" and "lost" camps is to give over forever to a certain questing part of you that will never, ever be at rest again.

In the old days they called going to California and getting embroiled in the mining excitement "going to see The Elephant." Perhaps because in those days the elephant was almost a mythical beast. Sure enough, it existed somewhere. People traveled for great distances to see it and once back from their journeys had great difficulty explaining where they had been and what they had seen. Hence "going to see The Elephant" has always been appropriate.

This is a slight breath, a mere puff of a magical smoke that is called ghost town exploring. They say that the one who breathes too deeply of such magical stuff stays gone from home and work for longer and longer periods of time as one grows older; that a sly twinkle in the eye only brightens with age; and that the store of stories about the fabulous ghost camps that have been seen and the even more fabulous camps that are being searched only grows longer and longer. Let the quest be long and gentle.

Chapter 1

How It All Started
The Legend of '49

"Seeing The Elephant" was a term heard often during the years of 1849-1859, the period of the great California Gold Rush. The phrase was used by those who dreamed of the instantaneous wealth that was believed could be found in California's virgin earth and her mighty rivers.

When the news of fabulous strikes throughout the Mother Lode reached far away places, thousands of gold seekers left home and family to join in this incredible adventure. The barren, placid state soon became one of the most bustling, populous areas in the West.

Before 1848 Mexico ruled over California, a remote region isolated from the urbane world of the East by 1,800 miles of scorching desert and impassible mountains. By sea it was 18,000 miles via Cape Horn. Spaniards and Mexicans settled the coastal lands on tracts donated to them by the Mexican government. The inland area was the domain of Indians and a few settlers who also had been granted estates by the government.

Among those settlers was Captain John Sutter who had been fortunate enough to obtain approximately a full 11 leagues of land (spanning 60 miles in length) from Governor Alvarado of Mexico. Sutter, being somewhat of a visionary and possessing a gifted tongue, managed to receive most of what he desired with minimal trouble. Enchanted with Sutter's personality, Alvarado not only promised him Mexican citizenship but also commissioned him to become "representative of the government and officer of justice on the Northern frontier."

With uncanny foresight, Sutter began building a fortress on his land in the Sacramento Valley which, appropriately, was to become known as Sutter's Fort. But, it was more than just a fort; it also provided a stopping place and home for many foreigners and Americans who traveled to California, eventually becoming the mecca of the overland pilgrimages.

Sutter engaged in a variety of projects, including his cattle ranch, fur trade and trapping and the construction of an irrigation system.

With the influx of immigrants over the years the community around the fort grew rapidly. Lumber was much in demand and Captain Sutter agreed to supply the necessary capital for a community sawmill. The site chosen was some 45 miles northeast of the fort, located on the south fork of the American River in the town of Coloma.

During the course of its construction Sutter's carpenter, James Marshall, discovered a problem with the tailrace on the mill. It was early in the morning of January 24, 1848 while checking the tailrace that Marshall noticed an object shining in a foot of water at the bottom of a ditch. He reached down and picked it up, and his heart began to thump wildly as he realized he was holding a gold nugget.

Sutter planned to keep the find a secret for as long as possible, knowing very well that he could become an extremely wealthy man. The ever loyal Marshall remained faithful to his employer and the two of them did their best to obtain more land without raising suspicion. Although they were unsuccessful in their goal and word of the discovery finally did leak out, few people took it seriously.

It wasn't long before a shrewd businessman by the name of Sam Brannan came to the conclusion that the more people who heard about gold in Coloma, the more supplies they would have to buy from his general store to outfit themselves with in their search for the magical color. With that thought in mind, Brannan filled a small bottle with several bright, golden nuggets and rode up and down Montgomery Street in San Francisco yelling, "Gold, gold from the American River!"

Upon hearing his energetic proclamation the residents of San Francisco took to the hills with gold fever. Before long, nearly everyone had deserted their homes and fields to join in the search. Reports of the "easy pickings" had almost depopulated coastal towns by the end of the year.

The once prosperous and gregarious Sutter was left behind sick and almost destitute. Having spent large sums of money on the sawmill in Coloma and on a gristmill at Brighton, he found himself alone with no one to operate them, nor to care for him in his time of need.

The property where Sutter's Fort stood was overrun and destroyed by hordes of gold seekers. All those who had Sutter's kindness bestowed upon them, in the end, deserted him in their lust for gold. Sutter was ultimately granted an annual pension of $3,000 by the State of California.

The gold rush of 1848 was strictly local. *Argonauts* (the name given to those who came to California in search of gold) dipped in and out of the rivers and scoured the shores for her bounty. Tools were non-existent but that was no deterrent. Isaac Humphrey, a professional miner from Georgia, reached the discovery site on March 9, 1848. He constructed a rocker for gold separation which was copied by hundreds until some even more efficient devices —arrastras, Long Toms and sluice boxes were developed. A quarter million dollars in gold was pried from California's earth before the arrival of winter.

Word of the ease in which fortunes were being made spread like wildfire. A Frenchman named Claude Chana had been on his way to meet his friend James Marshall at the Coloma diggings when he and his party decided to stop for a while at Auburn Ravine. Practicing with his mining pan, Chana immediately came up with three good-sized nuggets and the party decided then and there to remain at the site. (Chana can be credited with having planted the first orchard in California — almonds and fruits, the seeds for which had been carried across the plains).

The town of Auburn was established in 1849 and the ravine became one of the richest in the world. In addition to its richness, this community was the center of extensive stage, freight and mining operations. The camp became an important trading center and supply depot for surrounding mines and stagecoach terminus. Here the "art" of stagecoach robbery had its beginning.

With all this talk and excitement that surrounded the newly-found territory, easterners still did not believe the rumors that drifted across the country of the enormous amount of wealth in the land. However, in President Polk's State-of-the-Union message on December 5, 1848 he declared; "The accounts of the abundance of gold in that territory are of such an extraordinary character as would scarcely command belief." It was with this announcement that gold fever became an international epidemic.

Some took ships, some wagons and others made the long journey on foot. No matter what their means of transportation, in 1849 more than 100,000 people poured into California. Gold was so plentiful that first summer, it was thought it would never end. Mines were free of crime and an abundance of gold along the American River waited in majestic silence to be discovered.

1848 had been a time of comaraderie and trust among the men in the mining camps and crime had been almost unknown. But, the "age of innocence" ended with the '48ers. Life soon became brutal as gold was spent recklessly and all the vices money could buy began to surface. The camp store supplied the men with sardines, oysters and French champagne. Merchants selling basic supplies and tools raked the most profits. Shovels, picks and wash pans were sold at a 1500 percent mark-up.

Before long the field of mining operations spread rapidly from the initial point at Coloma to better diggings upstream and downstream.

Indians were employed quite often by the more enterprising businessmen to dig gold for them, being repaid for their efforts with cheap trinkets. A kidney-shaped nugget was produced by Chief Jose Jesus which weighed 80½ ounces. His men were then sent to the Stanislaus River where new and richer diggings were opened.

At each site, gold seemed to bubble up from the earth and flow out of the water. No one who traveled to the Mother Lode thought they'd ever be poor again. And they came in droves. It was apparent that California's charming, idyllic way of life was gone forever.

As waves of homesteaders and would-be miners descended on California in 1849, the crowded trails posed hazards all their own. Cholera and scurvy ran rampant through the '49ers' camps. Pack animals faced starvation since the grass supply had been eaten by the animals that had traversed the route before them. The lure of gold, however, drove the travellers on.

By the time the Territorial Convention assembled, California had become so wealthy and populated that the recommendation of its becoming a territory was bypassed in favor of it being admitted to the Union as a state, which occurred in 1850.

Within four years after the Spring of 1849 the population of the state was 300,000. More than $260 million had been dug from the gold fields.

It was 1850 before gold was found in the town of Columbia. During the exploration, a shovel was stuck into a hill and 30 pounds of nuggets were instantly removed. As usual, this caused a rush to the new area and, immediately, a mining camp was established.

The Wells Fargo Express Company, housed in a two-story brick structure with iron shutters and fancy grillwork, was opened in Columbia in 1858. Wells Fargo weighed out $55 million in gold over the years, using scales so precise the miners claimed, "They could show the weight of a pencil mark on paper." The town's topsoil gave up almost $90 million in gold. But, by 1860 the easily mined placer gold had just about been depleted.

When easily accessible gold deposits were exhausted, most communities experienced either rapid population decline or were totally abandoned. Columbia's population of 20,000 plummeted to a mere 500.

There were many ways gold made itself known to the men: One prospective miner pitched a tent and in the morning, when he pulled out the stake, he unearthed several large nuggets. Others had boiled fish in a pot for dinner and, while the pot was being cleaned, they found it to be laden with gold.

A storekeeper from Angels Camp, Bennager Raspberry, was having problems with a rifle that had been jamming on him. He tried to fix it by shooting it into the ground. The bullet ricocheted and hit a rock, breaking it open to reveal a sizable gold deposit. Within three days he scraped $10,000 worth of gold dust out of the rocky ground.

This is the area where the term "Mother Lode" first came into usage in 1851. It refers to the *Veta Madre* which the Mexicans claimed existed. From it a series of veins supposedly sprouted and extended along the western slope of the Sierras (passing right through Angels Camp).

Angels Camp is also notable for attracting such famous personalities as writers Mark Twain and Bret Harte. Twain lived in a modest cabin in the town, but it was Harte who admitted he disliked the rough life of mining camps and found the foothills "ugly, vulgar and lawless."

For awhile the idea of becoming a miner, and one who could become fabulously wealthy overnight, led thousands of romantics to the golden state. It didn't take long before reality set in and the dreamers realized that gold mining was a back-breaking business with most of the waking hours being spent in search of the precious metal.

When time was found for relaxation, the men amused themselves by dancing, drinking, gambling and staging bull and bear fights. Longing for some culture to be put back into their lives, they revelled in delight when the theatre made its way to the mines. A regular circuit of players including Lola Montez, Lotta Crabtree and Edwin Booth, entertained the men.

Lola Montez (also known as the mistress of the King of Bavaria) made her home in Grass Valley from 1853-1855. A unique woman, Lola shared her home with her husband Patrick Hull, an editor of the *San Francisco Whig*, and her pet bear. Needless to say, she was not very popular with her neighbors. But, her beautiful figure, flashing eyes and ravenblack hair captivated audiences wherever she performed. Her best known act was the Spider Dance in which rubber spiders were sewn to her costume and were shaken out as she danced "in perfect rhythm to the clicking of castanets."

It was during her stay in Grass Valley that Lola discovered the young Lotta Crabtree and, without hesitation, took her under her wing. With Lola's tutelage, Lotta soon became the darling of the miners. Because of the scarcity of women in the camps, the hardened men went wild over Lotta as the eight-year-old danced a vigorous Irish Jig. In appreciation they showered her with coins and nuggets.

After a while the theatre moved on and Lola returned to San Francisco with little success. In 1861, at the age of 42, she died in poverty in New York. Lotta, however, continued to perform, enjoying a very successful career.

One starry night in Grass Valley, during October 1850, George McKnight stumbled on a shiny rock poking out of the ground. Close examination revealed that the rock was loaded with gold.

It was this find that has been declared California's second great gold discovery. Up until now, all of this precious metal had been found in free form and usually near water. Here was "gold in place."

In order to extract the gold from hard rock, stamp mills were soon brought into the Mother Lode. It was California's miners who made many improvements to the mills, thereby making the state the major ore processor in the gold region.

After the mid-1850s, production never again reached that of the peak year of 1852, when gold worth $81,294,700 was taken out of California's mines. In 1880, after other placers were developed, production again soared. But, it was mining companies rather than individual miners that raised the necessary capital for shaft tunneling and timbering through bedrock, and for heavy machinery and hoses in the case of hydraulic operations.

The Empire Mine, the largest and richest in Grass Valley, plunged 3500 feet into the earth. When the miners descended in a car they left the headframe at 800 feet per minute. From 1850 until 1956, the Empire complex recorded more than $75 million in gold as having been sent to the mint. The Empire was the longest operating gold mine in California.

But, as with everything in life, nothing lasts forever. The enormous amount of gold which emerged throughout the Mother Lode would eventually dwindle.

J.J. Ott's assay office in Nevada City had served the miners well since 1855. Four years later a man stopped by the office with a sample of blue clay from the Washoe Hills in the state of Nevada. It had been clogging the miners' rockers. Ott made test after test and could scarcely believe the results. The sample proved to be an exceedingly rich silver sulphide assaying at $3,000 a ton silver and another $800 in gold.

This discovery led to the Comstock Silver rush to Virginia City, Nevada. It didn't take long before this camp became the richest mining town in the world.

On August 10, 1885, 37 years after his discovery of gold in Coloma, James Marshall's body was found fully clothed on his bed in a small room in the Union Hotel in Kelsey. He had never again found gold, and earned pin money by selling his autograph. During his lifetime he had been sneered and laughed at and mistrusted by many who had "seen The Elephant." He died an embittered, lonely man in a city only five miles from Coloma.

But, the impact Marshall's discovery had on California was not forgotten. High on a hilltop overlooking the American River is a monument erected in his behalf. A bronze figure of him points to the spot of his initial gold find. James Marshall's body lies in peace beneath the monument.

Chapter 2

The Mother Lode

While the first recorded discovery of gold in California took place at Placerita Canyon, Los Angeles County in 1842, that finding by one Francisco Lopez did not cause much excitement. Today at that site there is a plaque and a rural county park. Annual ceremonies are held.

Historians record that the following year, in 1843, California gold production reached 2000 ounces, value $38,000.

The REAL discovery, the BIG discovery of gold took place six years later halfway up the state. On January 24, 1848, at Sutter's Mill on the American River, a place that would eventually be called Coloma, in El Dorado County, John Marshall found gold in the millrace and the stampede to California began. It has not yet ceased.

Neither Sutter nor Marshall became wealthy because of the find.

Gold seekers came from all over the world, some from as far away as Chile and Australia.

This incident on the American River was the start of the Gold Rush. It was the focus around which the Mother Lode developed until it included parts of nine California counties: Mariposa, Tuolumne, Calaveras, Amador, El Dorado, Placer, Yuba, Nevada and Sierra. The Mother Lode involves the drainages of at least seven major Sierra rivers, including the Merced, Tuolumne, Stanislaus, Mokelumne, Consumnes, American and Yuba.

The "Mother Lode Highway" — State Highway 49 — starts at the south at Oakhurst and runs north to Sattley. State Highway 49, also known as "The Golden Chain", and its side roads — not including the mountain passes — that run back to all manner of mine and town sites is about 300 miles in length.

There can be no firm estimate of the number of ghost towns related to the Gold Rush in the Mother Lode because of the simple reason stated elsewhere in this book: Historians cannot agree on just precisely what IS a ghost town. Several scholarly books list hundreds.

No matter how many, there are enough mine sites, vanished and moribund, alive and lively camps across the Mother Lode to delight ghost town buffs for an eternity.

Perhaps the grandest is the restored California State Historic Park in the community of Columbia. Perhaps the place with the most "mood" is either Murphy's or Volcano. Perhaps the one best

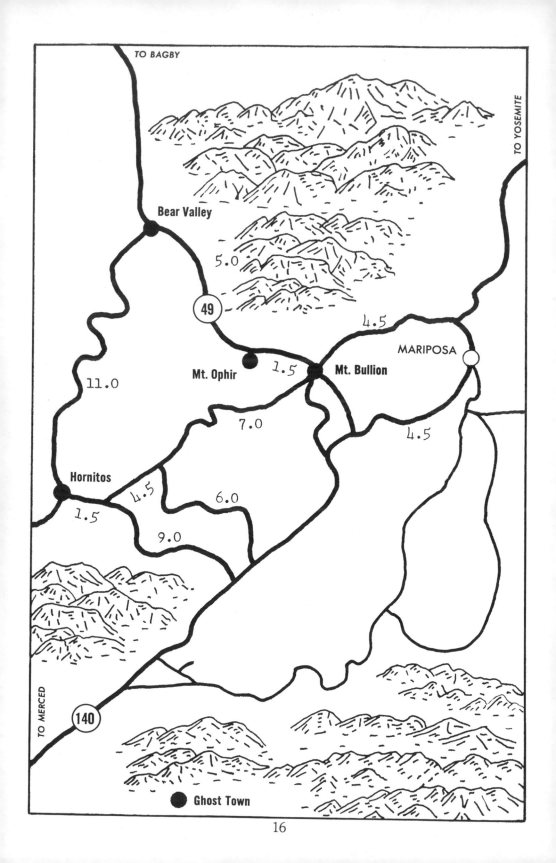

TO BAGBY

TO YOSEMITE

Bear Valley

5.0

49

4.5

Mt. Ophir

1.5

Mt. Bullion

MARIPOSA

11.0

7.0

4.5

Hornitos

4.5

6.0

1.5

9.0

TO MERCED

140

● Ghost Town

16

perpetualized by a famous writer is Angels Camp (Mark Twain's *The Celebrated Jumping Frog of Calaveras County*). Perhaps the most exciting ghost camp is Alleghany, clinging to a mountainside, a town built on the bias, above the deep ravine of Kanaka Creek.

Many of the camps had colorful names which often bespoke the kind of a camp it had been: Pleasant, Worthy, Murderous, A Bonanza, Hangtown, Second Garrotte, Happy Valley, Starvation Flat.

The totally, completely, simplest way to see the Mother Lode is to start at either Oakhurst or Mariposa and drive State Highway 49 north. There isn't much to see between Oakhurst and Mariposa in the way of old mining camps, and Mariposa is easier to reach. However, if you want to sew on your "merit badge sash" that you have been to Ahwahnee and Nipinnawasee, you'd better start at Oakhurst. It's a charming little town, so you can't lose.

As you drive north along Highway 49 — and off from side to side here and there — you'll get the feel of the place. You'll find silliness, jimcrack souvenir shops, antique shops that have local and imported antiques, mixed with enjoyable places to browse and eat and play tourist.

In the back country you'll find people still looking for gold. And, there are tumbled down buildings dating back to the Depression of the 1930s, or the real old Gold Rush days.

There is the old locomotive on view at Coulterville which the kids will love. The old hotel at Georgetown, the stone buildings with iron shutters (so many town-destroying fires consumed the camps in those early days). You'll find Masonic Halls and ruins of Masonic Halls — all had to be two stories tall, you know. Upstairs the secret meetings were held.

You'll find stone buildings with dates on them in iron or stone. You'll see the giant tailing wheels behind Jackson (and some fine restaurants nearby). You'll see the restored mill at Coloma and the statue on the hill.

You'll discover an incredible freeway linking Grass Valley and Nevada City, built for reasons that some have yet to puzzle out. However, the excavation in one town or the other for the freeway segment uncovered the burial ground of enough antique bottles to make wealthy a number of local collectors.

You can find more than one covered bridge, some marvelous, enormous, incomprehensible machineries; bits of stamp mills and ball mills and other hardware.

By the time you've reached Downieville, the air is always winey and the woodsmoke smell from the loggers' sawdust burners is a perpetual sweet perfume. You can stop at Herrington's Sierra Pines Resort at Sierra City and have a fine dinner in a fine dining room, then spend the

BEAR VALLEY — *This town was built in the 1850's by Col. Fremont as headquarters for the large mining operations being conducted on his 44,000 acre estate. The town reached a peak population of 3,000. Fremont paid $3,000 for the grant in 1847 and sold the entire grant in 1863 for $6 million.*

A few people still live here, as they do in most of the mining towns along Highway 49. The old Bon Ton Saloon still stands, along with the stone walls of stores with iron doors and shutters which are so familiar in the Mother Lode Country.

night in a motel wing built delightfully on the very edge of the Yuba River where the river's thunder almost precludes conversation, but lulls you to sleep like an angelic choir. A place to pause and regroup, study maps, fatten on fresh air and the scoldings of jays and sweet fresh mountain water, and move on to the end of Highway 49.

For those of you who would like to "collect" some famous mountain

HORNITOS — *Settled in 1850 by lawless minors who were ousted from Quartzburg, it was considered to be one of the wildest little towns in the area. It eventually reached a population of 15,000, and was reputed to be a hideout for the infamous bandit, Joaquin Murrieta.*

The first Wells Fargo office in the county was situated here, and $44,000 worth of gold was shipped out every day. Several of the old buildings that were built around 1860 are still in use, including the jail, but a lot of the store buildings are crumbling. The big heavy iron doors and shutters are quite plentiful throughout this area and some can still be seen at Hornitos.

passes while you are in the Mother Lode Country, the pickings are good. And, the passes are historic. Along at least one of them, the Sonora, Forest Rangers mention that they have found brief runs of an old emigrant-day corduroy road laid down so that wagons could more easily make the mountain crossing.

Along another one, the Donner, the highway runs parallel to the railroad, that incredible railroad, the western arm being built toward the eastern arm and meeting at Promontory Point in Utah.

In spots along Donner Pass Road, Highway 80, you can see the snow sheds built for the trains. More than once, in years past, streamliners have been stuck in the snow in Donner Pass.

The Yuba Pass Road runs parallel to a boisterous, noisy river much of the way. The old Mother Lode Gold Rush town of Downieville straddles the river. And, yep, it has been flooded.

But for Sierra Pass collectors, each with its supply of Mother Lode ghost camps along the way, from south to north, they are:

Tioga Pass, which runs mostly through the back country of Yosemite National park (all the pass roads can be closed by snow in the winter) and has a dramatic descent on the eastern end into the Lee Vining Country. Summit: 9941 feet.

Moving north, Sonora Pass takes off from the big town of Sonora and ambles and climbs slowly. But, once it gets into the high country, it is spectacular. This one drops down on the east side near Bridgeport, into Mono County, along the Walker River. The U.S. Marine Corps cold weather training base is on that eastern descent at Pickel Meadows. Summit: 9624 feet.

Next to the north is Ebbetts Pass. This one drifts sort of casually out of the Angels Camp country and provides one back-door route into the south end of Lake Tahoe via Markleeville, Alpine County seat. Some nice ghost camps are found coming down the hill to the Pass's end. Summit: 8730 feet.

On north to Carson Pass. This one starts at Jackson on Highway 49 and almost immediately is in delicious country. It ends between Markleeville and the south end of Lake Tahoe. Summit: 8600 feet.

Up to now these have been pretty gentle, not always freeway-wide mountain roads, all closed by winter and most of them left that way with no big effort to keep them open.

Starting with the next one north, Highway 50, the Echo Pass Road, the byway is more serious about getting from Placerville to the south end of Lake Tahoe. Effort is made to keep it open. Lots of skiers use it. Summit: 7382 feet.

Interstate 80, which runs from Auburn to Truckee and on into Reno, is usually kept open, if possible, in the snowy season. It summits at Donner Pass, 7135 feet.

North still, an extension of Highway 49 itself becomes the Yuba Pass Road, running past the turnoff up to delightful cliff-edge Alleghany, and down to old French Corral and the covered bridge at Bridgeport. It has its summit at 6701 feet.

Of course the way to see the Mother Lode is to set goals. Make up your mind to see the big tailing wheels at Jackson Gate, or the covered bridge at Knight's Ferry, the iron-shuttered towns of Murphy's and Volcano. Drive Highway 49 from Oakhurst to the end at Sattley. Drive all the seven mountain passes. And then ask ten people you meet along the way their favorite Mother Lode site and include that in what you see.

The lower elevations of the Mother Lode can get quite warm by summer; and conversely quite chilly by winter.

Most of the year, most of the places, the Mother Lode is a sheer delight, a surprise around every turn. The easy places to find along Highway 49 are sometimes touristy, but sometimes you find it still rich with the pervasive wood smoke-like odor of yesterday.

Look for old timers, people with roots in the area. Even if they were born there in the 1920s, they will have splendid tales to tell of things they have found, places they have seen that are gone now, and old timers that THEY once knew who had been born, perhaps, in that same area a generation earlier still. A kid in Volcano in the 1930s just could possibly have known an old timer, in his eighties, who had lived in the area when the big excitement was still on the land.

Of course, the wandering-off side roads are usually more fun. The time of day, the time of year, the cast of sun and shadow will make your own visit special.

If following a logging truck down a narrow dirt road steep hill puts too much diesel fumes in the air for you, pull off the road, get out, and walk around and look at the country until that wash of exhaust blows away. You just might stumble onto a special vista, a part of an old building, or as happened with us one day, a spread of soft earth upon which we found all manner of fresh animal tracks. Some were little critters, like ground squirrels or pikas, some were larger, maybe rabbits. There were many deer tracks and some were big and smudged — from some critter larger still. A bobcat? We spent a long time playing animal trackers and quite forgave the diesel logger we had been following down the narrow mountain road.

Take pictures and ask questions.

An addiction to this country is like the one kind of measles they tell you about. You can suffer it more than once. It is an itch that comes back from time to time and the only kind of soothing syrup that helps at all is just to go back again.

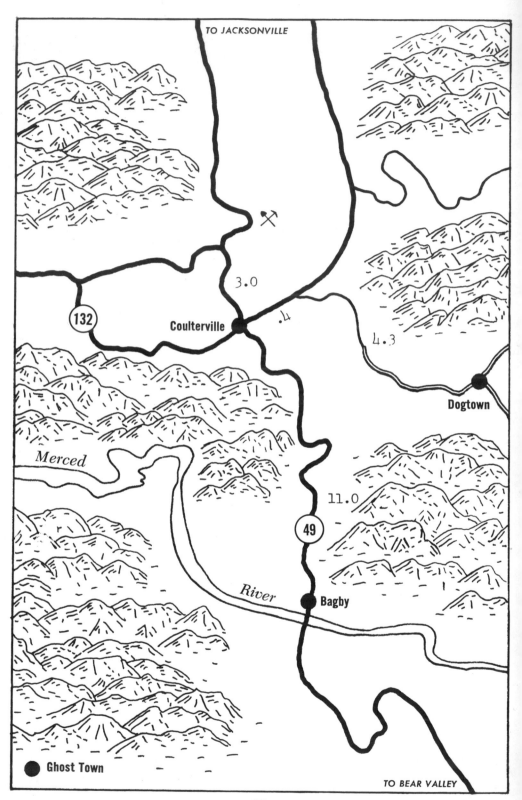

TO JACKSONVILLE

132

Coulterville

Dogtown

Merced

River

Bagby

3.0

.4

4.3

11.0

49

● Ghost Town

TO BEAR VALLEY

22

COULTERVILLE — Originally called Bandereta.

Many of the old buildings are still occupied. The Wells Fargo Building has been turned into a museum and the one remaining building in the Chinatown section is still in use. The saloon and fandango hall built in 1851 are still standing, along with several other old buildings and a large oak "hangmans tree."

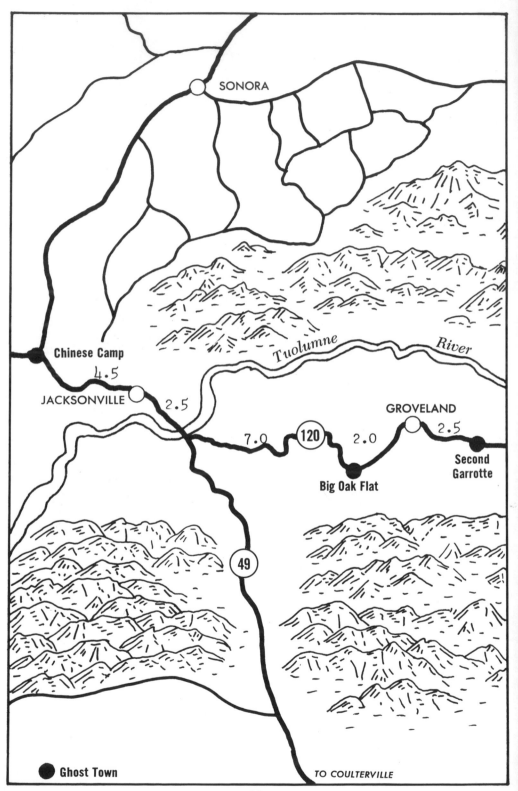

SONORA

Chinese Camp

4.5

JACKSONVILLE

2.5

7.0 120 2.0

Big Oak Flat

GROVELAND

2.5

Second
Garrotte

Tuolumne   *River*

49

● **Ghost Town**

TO COULTERVILLE

SECOND GARROTTE — This site is characterized by Hangman's Tree, an old oak tree which is reputed to have served in 60 hangings. An old cabin nearby, built in 1853, is called the "Bret Harte Cabin," but there is no evidence that Bret Harte ever lived there.

Groveland, 2 miles west, was originally called Garrote, being the first so named because a horse thief was hanged there. There has always been an argument about the spelling of the two camps.

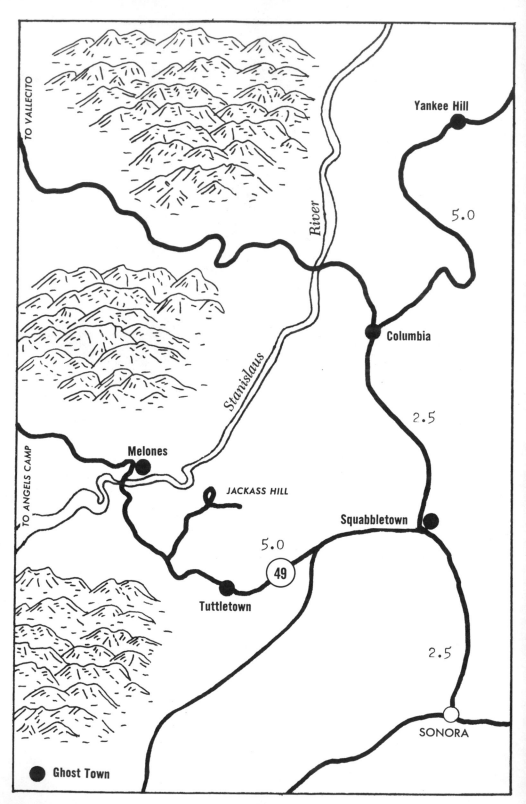

TO VALLECITO

Yankee Hill

5.0

River

Columbia

2.5

Stanislaus

Melones

JACKASS HILL

TO ANGELS CAMP

Squabbletown

5.0

49

2.5

Tuttletown

SONORA

● Ghost Town

COLUMBIA — *A well preserved ghost town, made into a State Historic Park in 1945.*

Gold was discovered in 1850 and in six weeks the population exploded to 6,000, continuing to boom until it reached a peak of 20,000. It was called one of the wickedest, toughest and richest mining towns in the West, with 40 saloons, 143 faro games, 27 general stores and an arena for bear fights. Ninety million dollars in gold was taken from the gravels here.

The Wells Fargo Office, saloons, firehouses, Masonic Temple and many old buildings erected in the 1850's are still standing and well preserved. Some buildings have been restored.

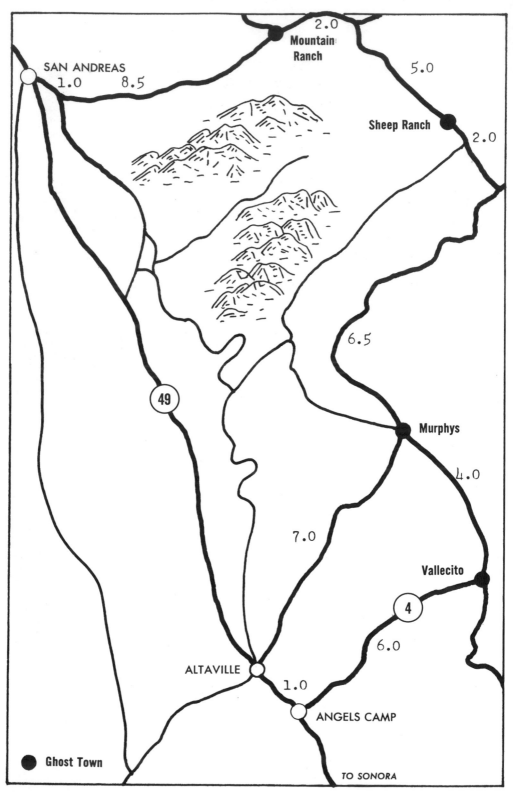

2.0
Mountain
Ranch

SAN ANDREAS
1.0   8.5

5.0

Sheep Ranch

2.0

6.5

49

Murphys

4.0

7.0

Vallecito

4

6.0

ALTAVILLE

1.0

ANGELS CAMP

● Ghost Town

TO SONORA

JACKSON GATE — Among the most photographed sights in the middle portion of the Mother Lode Country are the giant tailing wheels at the old Kennedy Mine near the town of Jackson. The succession of wheels helped haul the debris from the deep hard rock mine shafts away from the diggings. (Nearby, today, is a row of excellent restaurants.)

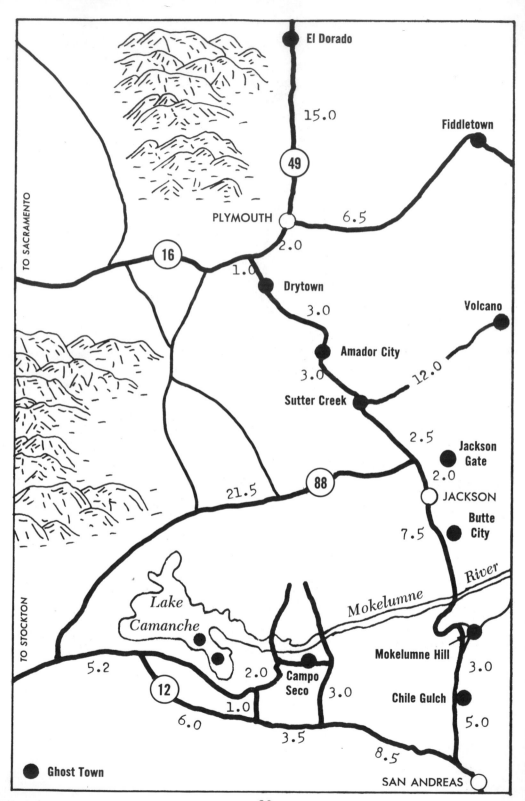

El Dorado

15.0

49

Fiddletown

6.5

PLYMOUTH

2.0

16

1.0

Drytown

3.0

TO SACRAMENTO

Volcano

Amador City

3.0

12.0

Sutter Creek

2.5

Jackson
Gate

88

2.0

21.5

JACKSON

Butte
City

7.5

Mokelumne River

Lake
Camanche

TO STOCKTON

Mokelumne Hill

3.0

5.2

2.0

Campo
Seco

3.0

Chile Gulch

12

1.0

5.0

6.0

3.5

8.5

Ghost Town

SAN ANDREAS

MOKELUMNE HILL — A rich gold placer deposit was discovered in the Mokelumne River in 1848 and miners flocked in to wash the rich gravels. The town started with one tent and quickly mushroomed to a population of 12,000 people. Mok Hill, as it is called by the old-timers, was a rough, tough town and at one period, it is rumored that a man was killed every weekend for 17 weeks, except for one weekend when 5 were killed.

CAMANCHE — *Only divers can reach Camanche now. The Camanche Dam was built on the Mokelumne River in 1963, flooding 7,700 acres of plains, canyons, gulches, and ravines. The old towns of Camanche, Lanhca Plana, and China Flat are all under water now. Several other old camps and town sites were also inundated by the rising waters.*

Lake Camanche is now a recreation area with fishing, swimming, water skiing, and good campgrounds.

VOLCANO — This town got a slow start but eventually reached a population of 8,000. Miners panning the gravel averaged $100 per day and some as much as $500. The gravel in the surrounding area produced $90 million in gold. Some of the town was undermined by gold diggers and collapsed. More of it was washed away by hydraulic mining, but many of the picturesque old buildings are well preserved.

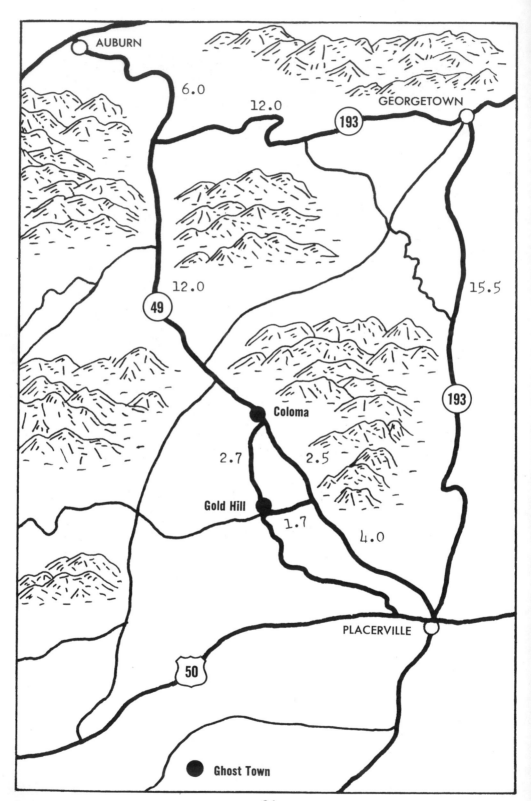

AUBURN

6.0

12.0

193

GEORGETOWN

12.0

49

15.5

Coloma

2.7

2.5

193

Gold Hill

1.7

4.0

PLACERVILLE

50

● Ghost Town

COLOMA — James Marshall discovered gold in the tailrace of John Sutter's sawmill at Coloma in 1848 and this started the great rush of argonauts over the westward trail to California. Coloma was the nucleus of the gold rush in California, the place where gold was discovered and the news made public to the world.

The remains of the old sawmill are now under water in the American River, but a replica of the mill has been erected on the shore next to Highway 49.

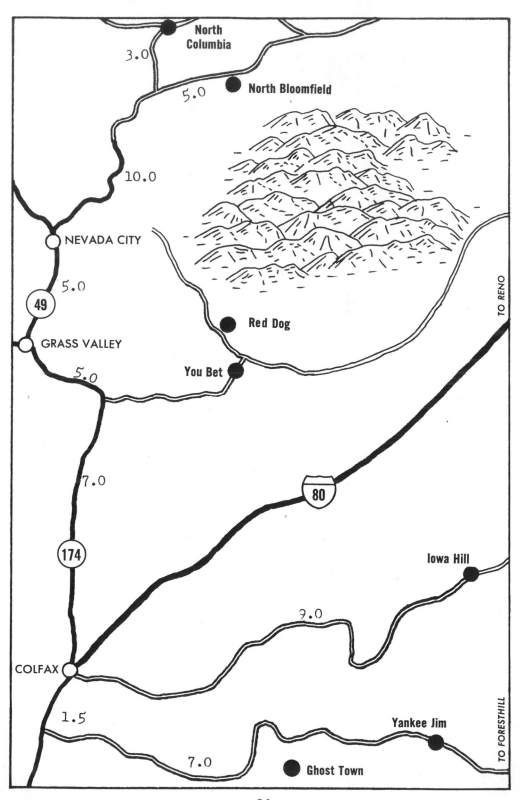

North
Columbia

3.0

5.0   North Bloomfield

10.0

NEVADA CITY

49   5.0

GRASS VALLEY

5.0   You Bet   Red Dog

7.0

174

80

Iowa Hill

9.0

COLFAX

1.5

7.0   Ghost Town   Yankee Jim

TO RENO

TO FORESTHILL

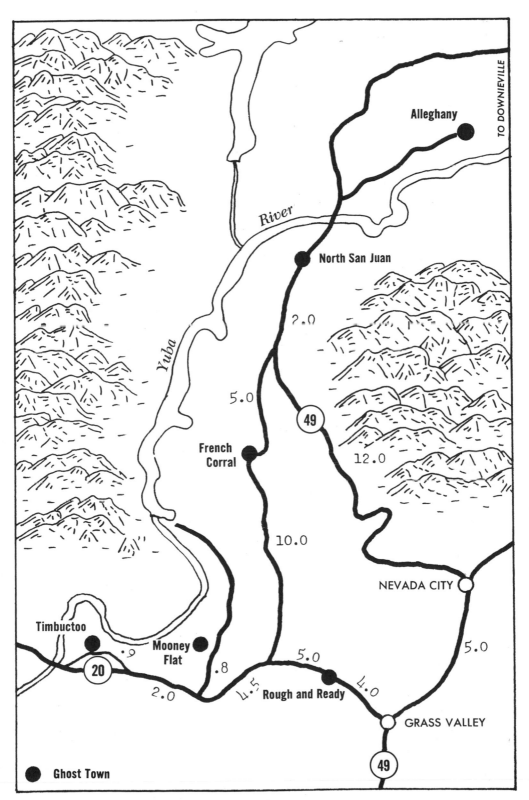

TO DOWNIEVILLE

Alleghany

River

North San Juan

2.0

Yuba

5.0

49

French
Corral

12.0

10.0

NEVADA CITY

Timbuctoo

Mooney
Flat

.9

5.0

5.0

20

.8

4.5

4.0

2.0

Rough and Ready

GRASS VALLEY

49

● Ghost Town

TIMBUCTOO — Setting on a hillside at a bend in the Yuba River, this old gold mining town was the largest in eastern Yuba County in 1865. Timbuctoo was a rough and lawless camp, and miners eventually moved away to better "diggings." The abandoned town was completely deserted for years and all that remains today is the shell of the old Wells Fargo building.

Chapter 3

The Big Ones

No serious historian would ever put his/her reputation on the line by estimating how many ghost towns there are in California. There are lots of them. The slippery part of the inability to put a number to them is because of the matter of definition. Just what is a ghost town? The same historians who will not estimate how many camps there are will not agree on what a ghost town is. How large? How long did it live before it ghosted? How many people lived there? Did it become a rich camp? Was it good or notorious? Did it ever have a post office? A store? A Lawman? A Newspaper? Ways of measuring the ghost towns of California vary.

Still, some were "big ones."

This book includes three favorites which have been called "big ones." They are tied together by history and geography:

None of them had anything directly to do with the Mother Lode or, directly, the Gold Rush.

Each of the camps, in its own time, lived at risk. One has been almost totally scrubbed away — largely by what some say is an angry Nature. One consists of three or four buildings today but at one time contributed significantly to the building of a metropolis. Fire touched here. One town is now a state park. At last count there were fifty odd buildings standing, ruins of more, sites of others. Most are identifiable. Fire visited here, too.

Each camp built a permanent reputation. These three big California ghost towns are: Bodie, a gold mine town, now a State of California Historic State park; Panamint City (the vanished); and Cerro Gordo (with only a handful of original buildings still standing). They are the finest of all the California ghost towns.

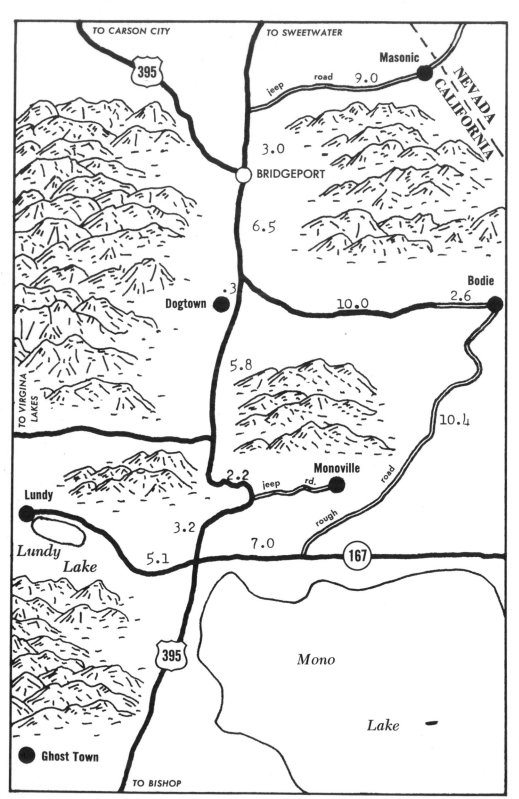

TO CARSON CITY

TO SWEETWATER

395

Masonic

jeep   road   9.0

NEVADA
CALIFORNIA

3.0

○ BRIDGEPORT

6.5

.3

Dogtown

10.0   2.6   Bodie

5.8

TO VIRGINA LAKES

10.4

2.2

Monoville

jeep   rd.

road

Lundy

rough

3.2

7.0   **167**

Lundy Lake

5.1

395

Mono

● Ghost Town

Lake   ▬

TO BISHOP

BODIE — Probably the most picturesque ghost town in California, this site is a State Historic Park. The town has been ravaged many times by fire, but many of the old wooden buildings are still standing, such as the fire house, school, saloon, livery stable, miners union hall and many others. A fine brochure is available at the park.

Though Bodie once boasted a population of 10,000, the only inhabitants now are the Park Rangers. It was a town, with many stage holdups right on the edge of the camp. The stage attracted bandits because it often carried gold bullion from the rich Bodie mines.

Bodie

To a ghost town addict, when the name "Bodie" is mentioned, the pulse picks up; there is a squirt of adrenaline. Aches vanish. One has a rush of visions . . . adventure looms.

Bodie was a town with a flavor all its own which probably can lay claim to more anecdotes than any other California ghost town. It was well chronicled. There was a newspaper that for a year and a half was published daily. Bodie anecdotes were often not the kind that got tacked onto just any mining camp.

The classic, however told, concerns the little girl who wrote a friend that she was moving away to a new, wicked, raw mining camp in Eastern California. In despair, the girl wrote a prayer to her friend.

"Goodbye, God," she is said to have written, "I'm going to Bodie."

In short order the editor of the Bodie newspaper heard the account of the young girl and her prayer. He is claimed to have investigated and reported in his publication that it was the *punctuation* that was at fault.

What the little girl had written, claimed the loyal Bodie newsman, was, "Good! By God I'm going to Bodie!"

Of such stuff was the legend of the camp born.

Bodie is situated in the high country of southern Mono County. It can be righteously hot by midsummer; buried in snows and whipped by winds down from the near-at-hand Sierra Nevada in wintertime.

The expression, "the bad man from Bodie" has a ring to it. It is doubtful, as some wags have suggested, that frontier mothers quieted their children at bedtime with a warning that "the bad man from Bodie" would get them, but without argument the expression has a raw, primitive charm . . . and has lasted. Historians argue over just which of Bodie's "bad men" was "the one."

Bodie possessed features many of the other frontier camps lacked. It had a large Chinese population and a rather extensive red light district. The mining was prodigious and the town which evolved was a conventional Western community in many ways. People moved here, men and women married, built wooden homes, started families, died and were buried here.

Bodie has a sizeable, impressive, perhaps unique cemetery to which there are three separate parts. The main part contains the remains and headstones for those folks who lived here, divided into some fraternal subsections. Some of the ornately carved marble cherub headstones for infant burials are heart-touching. The second part was for the Chinese, this was a segregated cemetery, you see. But there was also a third area, where the ladies of the evening — the prostitutes — were buried. As in many of the Western frontier camps, the generous-hearted prostitutes were often loved by the town's people for qualities far beyond the skills of their profession. Still, as a community, Bodie insisted that its painted ladies be buried apart.

Bodie had a railroad — the Bodie and Benton. It ran southeast, in search of wood for the Bodie smelters, then around the eastern edge of Mono Lake. It paused at the colorful ghost camp of Mono Mills, a

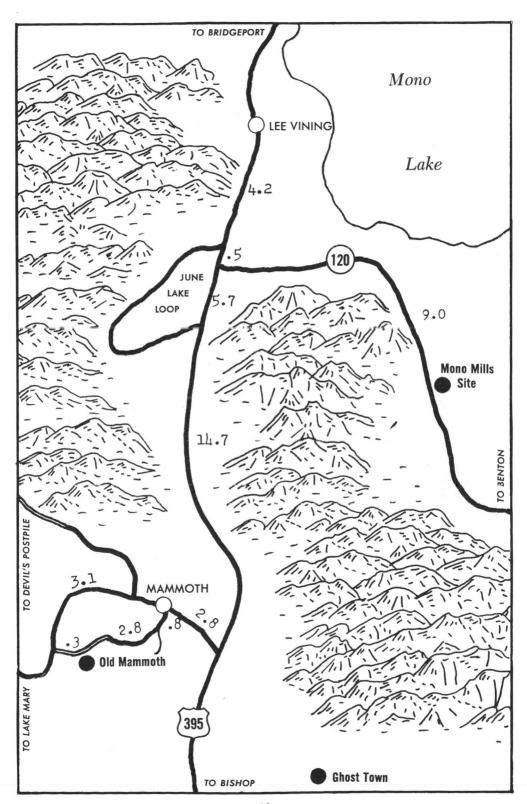

TO BRIDGEPORT

Mono

Lake

LEE VINING

4.2

.5

120

JUNE
LAKE
LOOP

5.7

9.0

Mono Mills
Site

14.7

TO BENTON

TO DEVIL'S POSTPILE

3.1

MAMMOTH

2.8

2.8

.3

.8

Old Mammoth

TO LAKE MARY

395

TO BISHOP

Ghost Town

MONO MILLS — A lumber and sawmill town, built about 1880 to supply the needs of the mining towns of Bodie and Aurora, about 30 miles to the north. The town folded up when Bodie closed her mines in 1914.

There are many fallen buildings and foundations scattered through the woods. Square nails are everywhere, and the huge timbers of the old mill are still hanging over the edge of the gulley where the mill set.

sawmill, an end-of-track-camp for a while. But, you can follow the old railroad roadbed on south from here, into the forest that lies just east of the line of the Mono Craters, into the deep woods, and then ... end of track.

The elevation of Bodie is 8400 feet. The camp was in deep snow by

MAMMOTH CITY — Situated in a beautiful setting high in the Sierra Nevada Mountains at an elevation of 9,000 feet. Gold was mined here from 1877 to 1881. The population in and around Mammoth City grew to 2,500. All that remains today are a few sunken foundations.

Mill City was located in the ravine below Mammoth City. The old town of Pine City was situated in the timber near Lake Mary.

winter. There was no easy route to civilization — to San Francisco or Los Angeles — out of Bodie. To San Francisco there was a mess of mountains to cross, which one seldom did by winter. Heading south, there was a lot of rough country before one gained the outskirts of Los Angeles.

The houses of Bodie were mainly timber. There were several bad fires and in more than one of these conflagrations it seemed that the entire town might burn. From the state parks office there you can obtain a brochure which includes a list of who lived where in the buildings that remain standing at Bodie.

You can walk through most of the town. It is a fascinating adventure. There are 13 miles of road, 10 of them paved, from Highway 395 into Bodie. Not everyone wants to drive the 13 miles, but they should. When it snows the road is closed.

Bodie, anyway you look at it, is perhaps the most important of the big ones. Visiting it is an adventure that stays with you for a long time.

Panamint City

You need an off-road vehicle to drive up Surprise Canyon to get to the site of Panamint City. It's a rough road.

There is not much there left to see except the ruins of the old 1875 brick smelter and chimney. Vandals have even whittled away at it.

It is a pity some legislator hasn't made an effort to preserve as much of Panamint City as possible. It could be part of the state park system; it could be added to Death Valley National Monument.

Panamint City came up in 1873-1874. The mines, mills, stores, saloons, red light district and the cemetery were built up along the uppermost fingers at the end of Surprise Canyon. It was a town scattered up a half dozen small side canyons, and each side canyon had its own flavor. One side canyon held the red light district, another the cemetery.

It was a rich town for a while, and if Bodie was isolated, this silver camp was just as far away from everything as Bodie would be; plus, it was stuck up at the end of a steep canyon on the West side of the Panamint Mountains. On the east side of the Panamints is Death Valley. Talk about isolated...

Bodie was considered a "tough" town. Panamint City was regarded

PANAMINT CITY — Rich silver deposits were discovered in Surprise Canyon in 1874 and Panamint City was born, quickly booming to a population of 2,000 people. It was a rough, tough, lawless town located at 6,640 feet elevation in the Panamint Mountains. Panamint City was devastated July 24, 1876 when a flash flood with a wall of water 20 feet high roared down the canyon, wiping out the town and several citizens. Within a year the camp was dead.

as "bad and wicked". It would come to no good, said those who hammered on their Bibles to make a point.

Shipments of silver down the canyon were constantly being hijacked by outlaws. Mine operators foiled the hijackers by casting each

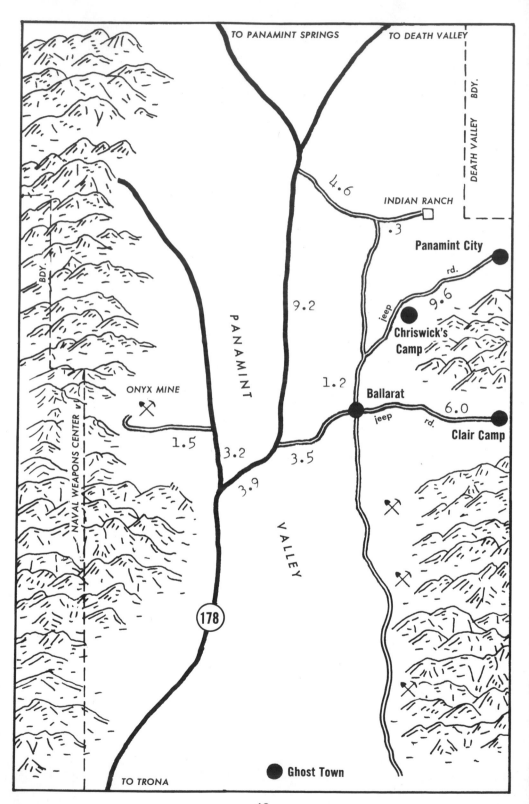

TO PANAMINT SPRINGS

TO DEATH VALLEY

DEATH VALLEY BDY.

4.6

INDIAN RANCH

.3

Panamint City

9.2

rd.

9.6

jeep

Chriswick's Camp

PANAMINT

ONYX MINE

1.2

Ballarat

6.0

jeep

rd.

Clair Camp

BDY.

NAVAL WEAPONS CENTER

1.5

3.2

3.5

3.9

VALLEY

178

TO TRONA

Ghost Town

48

BALLARAT — A gold mining town of the 1890's, situated in Panamint Valley at the base of the Panamint Mountains. A few buildings and walls are still standing.

For many years this old ghost town was the home of the late Frank "Shorty" Harris, well known Mojave Desert prospector. Another colorful character that lived here was an old prospector called "Seldom Seen Slim", real name Charles Ferge, who kept the forgotten Ballarat cemetery tidy.

wagonload of silver in one enormous blob of cast silver. It weighed too much for anyone on horseback to carry away.

Panamint City had a newspaper, boomed and lived through deeper winter snows than Bodie. On July 24, 1876, dark clouds moved in over the Panamints. The mountain country has always known heavy rain storms. All one has to do is study the enormous alluvial fans in Panamint Valley and Death Valley, stuff that has been washed by rainwaters down from the mountains.

On this day the "bad and wicked" city was hit by a prodigious rainstorm. A cloudburst. Waters gathered higher in the Panamints and came boiling down the individual canyons toward Panamint City.

The resultant flood scoured out the canyon that held the red light district; the canyon in which was situated the cemetery; the canyons that held the boarding houses, offices, homes, stores and saloons. Some

WILD ROSE CAMP — A view of a few of the ten masonry charcoal kilns built in the Panamints (where there was timber) to make charcoal for the silver smelters of the Coso mines in the Coso Mountains across the Panamint Valley to the west (where there was no timber). A small kiln community sprang up at Wild Rose.

of the pieces of Panamint City were sluiced all the way down and scattered across the Surprise Canyon alluvial fan that reaches out across the Panamint Valley. Other pieces of the old camp can still be found, rotting, rusted — boards spiked with square nails — junked, up there at the head of the canyon of silver.

Many were killed. Panamint City was dead by 1877. The Bible-pounders claimed that the "bad and wicked" town got what it deserved.

Today some of the townsite area is private property (do not trespass). There is a little mining going on. But you can still visit the ruins of the old smelter and chimney, and walk through the rubble of the flood...of the many floods...even.

Panamint City, was a big one, and bad one, one that we should have — maybe still can — save. Not much is left. But see it. It is important.

Cerro Gordo

Cerro Gordo *has* produced gold, but mostly silver. — A kind of silver-lead. The mines there on the side of the Inyo Mountains, just east of Owens Lake, produced enough of the metal that some historians have called it "the Comstock of Los Angeles." The wealth of Cerro Gordo helped build old Los Angeles. Even the freighter, Remi Nadeau, who hauled from camps all over the Mojave, made money from Cerro Gordo, enough at least that there once was a Nadeau Block and a Nadeau Hotel in that older Los Angeles.

Cerro Gordo was first discovered by Mexican prospectors, perhaps as early as 1865. It actually boomed about 1867-1868. A mine and a mill were built up on the hill. A tramway helped to haul the millings down the infamous Yellow Hill; mules and wagons did the heavy work. A smelter was built at Swansea, at the bottom of the grade. A town nearby, nearer the lake edge, Keeler, would be born.

Nadeau argued that the soft sand around the south edge of Owens Lake made freighting the ingots of silver lead too difficult, so two small lake steamers were built, the *Bessie Brady* and the *Mollie Stevens*. They hauled the ingots across placid, mountain-rimmed Owens Lake to the camp of Cartago, just north of Olancha. Here Nadeau's teams picked up the metal.

The smelters at Swansea needed charcoal and the Inyo Mountains were not densely forested. But, the Sierra Nevada, up the slope from Cartago to the west, was heavily pined. A mill was built high on the flank of the Sierra on Cottonwood Creek. (Until recently when arsonists and vandals changed all that, the ruins of the Cottonwood Mill still stood.) The wood was flumed down the hill into Cartago where a row of beehive charcoal kilns made the charcoal. When the steamers unloaded the ingots of metal, they loaded up with charcoal for the trip back to Keeler.

A narrow gauge railroad, called the Carson and Colorado, would eventually build into this country. It started at Mound House, outside Carson City, Nevada, and ended at Keeler, a long way from the Colorado River. In a manner of speaking, Keeler, a remote mountain community, was once both a steamboat town and a railroad terminal. Not bad for a town that itself is almost, but not really, ghosted today. The Carson and Colorado is gone. The smelter at Swansea is gone. The

51

steamers have disappeared; one burned dockside, one sank in mid-lake. The propeller from what might have been one of them was found some years back in Owens Lake. The Cottonwood Mill and most of the flume are gone. The charcoal kilns are in ruins; a couple exist behind chainlink fencing, a historical landmark. Cartago is gone. In fact, there are only the hotel and a couple of buildings left at Cerro Gordo. Even

CERRO GORDO — Rich outcroppings of silver-lead ore were discovered on the mountain in the 1860's and the town of Cerro Gordo boomed to a population of 2,000. About 150 bars of silver weighing 85 pounds each left the mine every 24 hours to be shipped across Owens Lake on the tiny steamers Bessie Brady and Mollie Stevens.

In the early 1900's an aerial tramway was built to carry the ore down the mountain to Keeler for shipping across the lake.

Cerro Gordo was always a wild lawless camp. Four of the original buildings remain in the old town. The eight mile climb up the mountain is very steep.

Owens Lake is gone. The water merchants in Los Angeles took that. What was once orchards, vineyards and grazing land is desert country today, pretty much all of it.

But Cerro Gordo's output was prodigious for a while. Then, like most of the boom camps, it "busted" and went under along with the rest.

As far as access to Cerro Gordo is concerned, the picture is unclear as this book goes to press. Property there is under patented mining claim, and there is talk of its being sold. Concerned parties who were contacted were not at liberty to give definite answers. Therefore, the future is indefinite. We can only advise that if you wish to visit this site that you check with authorities and merchants in Lone Pine and Keeler. Above all, be sure that you do not trespass should the property be closed. (If you should happen to be a rock hobbyist, we have been given to understand that the location has already been closed to mineral collecting.)

The road from Keeler up Yellow Grade to Cerro Gordo is maintained

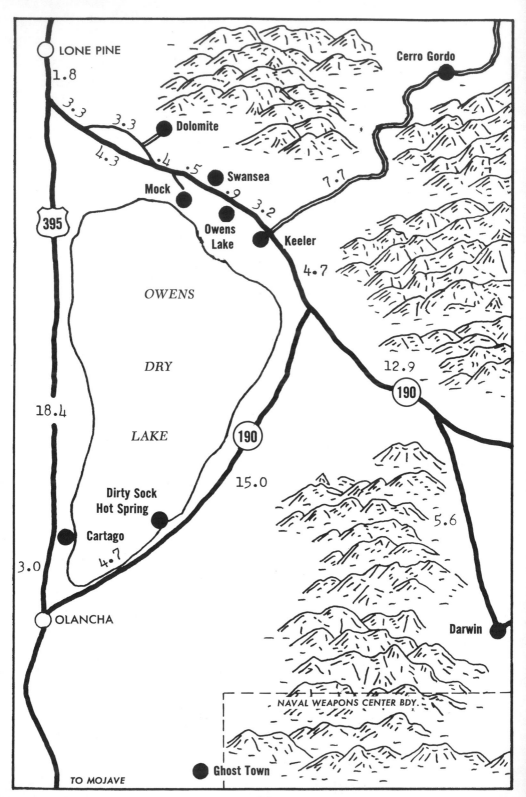

LONE PINE

1.8

3.3   3.3

4.3   .4   .5

Dolomite

Swansea

Mock   .9   3.2

Owens
Lake   Keeler

Cerro Gordo

7.7

395

4.7

OWENS

DRY

12.9

18.4

LAKE   190

190

15.0

Dirty Sock
Hot Spring   5.6

Cartago

4.7

3.0

OLANCHA   Darwin

NAVAL WEAPONS CENTER BDY.

Ghost Town

TO MOJAVE

54

by the County and is, therefore, public. It is a narrow dirt road of about 8 miles, the last few miles of which are very, very steep. Stock vehicles in good condition can make it, but four-wheel drive is much better. Before starting up this road, check about conditions; washouts have been known. Winter snows can make it impassable. The Sheriff's station at Lone Pine can provide current information.

(As a small sidelight, there are tales of *another* ghost town, somewhere deep in the Inyo Mountains behind Cerro Gordo, where, according to legend, the tools are still lying on the ground outside the miners' houses, and where furniture still stands inside the old deserted homes — a Shangri-La of a ghost town. It has become one of the more anecdotal, partially apocryphal, ghost camps in all the state. Yet, some folks in Owens Valley are said to have walked to the site — many times. It is also said that some individuals in Los Angeles who had heard the fabulous stories got there by helicopter and were almost killed getting out.) My suggestion, just collect the delicious anecdotes about this one. Its name? Ah yes, it was called Beveridge — ghost camp of many legends.

DOLOMITE — Named after the mineral that was mined here, the old town
sets on the desert floor at the base of the southern tip of the Inyo Mountains.
Several buildings are still standing, including the saloon. Stone quarrying is
still being done in the area.

SWANSEA — *This town was built in 1870 to support the nearby camp of Owens Lake. Some of the ore from Cerro Gordo was smeltered at the Owens Lake furnaces and most workers lived in Swansea. The walls and frames of several buildings still stand. Relic hunters prowl the old stone ruins.*

DARWIN — Rich silver-lead ores were discovered in 1874. A rush followed and the town of Darwin was established. By 1875 it had some 20 operating mines, 2 smelters, 200 frame houses and more than 700 citizens. A year later the population topped 1,000.

The town has never been completely deserted, but mighty close to it, and only a handful of residents remain today.

With the price of gold spiraling upward, some of the old mines around Darwin are being re-worked, bringing more people into the old town.

Chapter 4

The Death Valley Country

One might be on safe ground by saying that all ghost towns in California are somehow traceable back to the discovery of gold at Sutter's Mill. Many do actually lie in the Mother Lode; that connection is obvious and direct.

Then, of course, far too many prospectors came to California to seek a fortune in the Mother Lode. A quote of the day held that the latecomers "had best bring along their own rock to stand on." Some picked the wrong streamlet in the Mother Lode to prospect, or got discouraged and looked elsewhere in California. Subsequent gold strikes in California, like Holcomb Valley in the San Bernardino Mountains or the Julian rush in San Diego County, are direct, straight-line spinoffs.

Then there were people who came to California hoping to get rich and get cheap land, and while they didn't get caught up in the Mother Lode fever, they became involved in something else just as contagious. California has known booms in most of the common precious metals, and many other commodities, from redwood lumber to borax.

So California has ghost towns that were gold camps, silver diggings, quicksilver locations, tungsten camps, borax sources, logging camps, military outposts and Utopian colonies. Not many states in the Union can claim the same.

Part of the boom of mining in the Death Valley Country can be attributed to the fact that folks WERE coming to California to look for gold.

But the Death Valley '49ers, that band of hardnosed Midwesterners who, in July, 1849, hired Captain Jefferson Hunt in Salt Lake City to take them to California, inadvertently started the Death Valley boom. Most of the group, driving 100 out of 107 wagons, decided to take a shortcut once they were somewhere south of Salt Lake City. The guide told them he had been signed on to take them to California via San Bernardino, and that's what he was going to do. As long as one wagon wanted to go on, along the same agreed upon route, he would lead it south to San Bernardino. But, if they all wanted to go crazy and strike out due west to the gold field because of some crazy map, he'd go as a guide.

Now, taking shortcuts on the way to California was not held as a smart thing to do in those days. Not many years before, a wagon party from Illinois had gone for a quicker way to California and had taken "the Hastings cutoff." This was the tragic Donner party. The "shortcut" was just the opposite. The party arrived at the foot of the Sierra, exhausted, just as first snow fell. Most of them never made it, and horrors of the Donner episode terrified wagon trains for years after.

Those heading west were determined. Within three days the new map proved faulty. Sixty of the shortcut folks changed their minds and came hurrying back to play catch-up with Captain Hunt.

None of the folks who took the regular wagon train into San Bernardino and thence into the Central Valley had any major trouble. Some of them were actually in the Mother Lode by the time the shortcutters started getting out of Death Valley.

The shortcut map, of course, was humbug. The '49ers had to dismantle their wagons, lower them over cliffs, reassemble them, trudge forward, disassemble again and pull the wagons up cliffs. Twenty-odd wagons, now. The trekkers ran low on food and water for themselves and their oxen. They raided Indian food gardens and the Indians took cruel revenge.

By the time the '49ers had reached the far western edge of Death Valley they were exhausted, their animals were starved, dead. Indians harrassed them. Children and adults were starving and weakened. Most of them escaped, but the majority carried cruel scars and told stories, when they reached safety, of a hideous landscape.

But, one splinter group, on its way out, on foot, made a singular find. A man lost the sight to his rifle. At a mountain rest stop, probably somewhere in the Panamints, the members of the party spotted frequent pieces of silver ore with bits of bright metal sticking out. The man with the rifle fashioned himself a silver gunsight. All agreed it was a rich silver find, but all decided to push on. Someday, maybe, come back and . . .

Once into the more civilized parts of the new California this group told the story of their many travails and of the silver gunsight site. None of them had much luck in the gold fields. They and some of the people they talked to started sending search parties into the Panamint Country looking for what soon became "The Lost Gunsight Lode." No one — probably — has ever found it. At least no major silver strike has ever been made in the general area where the new silver gunsight was fashioned.

But, those people who came back, or who came to look based on the story, first-hand, second-hand, whatever, made other rich strikes in Death Valley, founded other camps.

Gold was found, towns were built, camps boomed, people poured in, towns went bust, people moved on. Silver was found and amazingly short-lived communities were built in the mountains, and died. Finally someone struck it rich, really rich, in Death Valley... This was the discovery of borax.

There were also copper camps. There was one camp built of nothing but snake oil and humbug.

And while the silver lode of the Lost Gunsight was being sought, all of the adjacent country was being walked by some one-blanket burro prospectors, the searchers who must have gone everywhere.

The mines of the Coso Range came up. Over in Nevada there was a string of fantastic gold discoveries — Rawhide, Goldfield; Candelaria; and the greatest silver camp of them all, Virginia City with its Comstock Lode.

In California an old site known by the Mexicans finally blossomed — Cerro Gordo. The Panamints had one whopper: Panamint City. It lasted four years. When the mines began to play out around Death Valley and the Cosos, the prospectors went north, and Aurora, Masonic, and another whopper — Bodie — boomed.

Many of the ghost towns in the Death Valley area today are within the boundaries of Death Valley National Monument. There was a time when off-roaders could go just about anywhere they wanted to in Death Valley. No more, and for good reason. There are many good ghost town sites in the area to visit, and the National Monument people (and others) provide all manner of aids: maps, illustrated lectures, helpful signs, wise and helpful rangers, fine museums, and pertinent regulations.

To many, Death Valley is the best portion of all of California to go ghost town hunting. Perhaps it is the romance of how it all came about. Perhaps it is the collection of colorful place names: the Funeral Mountains, Coffin Canyon, Skull Canyon. Maybe it is the stark, contrasting beauty of the place. Within Death Valley National Monument is the lowest point in the Continental United States at Bad Water. From Dante's View in Death Valley you can see the not-too-distant jagged spire of Mount Whitney, the highest mountain in the Lower 48.

Give it this. Death Valley is room enough. By spring the wildflowers may rival the best in the West. By summer it has reached 136 degrees, and it has been, "unofficially," many degrees hotter than that.

KEANE WONDER MINE — The ruins of the Keane Wonder Mill and tramway inside Death Valley National Monument mark one of the old-time big producers that visitors can see today on a trip to the National Monument. Other Death Valley mines of interest are the Old Lila C., a borax producer; the copper mines at Furnace and Greenwater; and Leadfield, which was, pure and simple, a swindle and produced nothing at all.

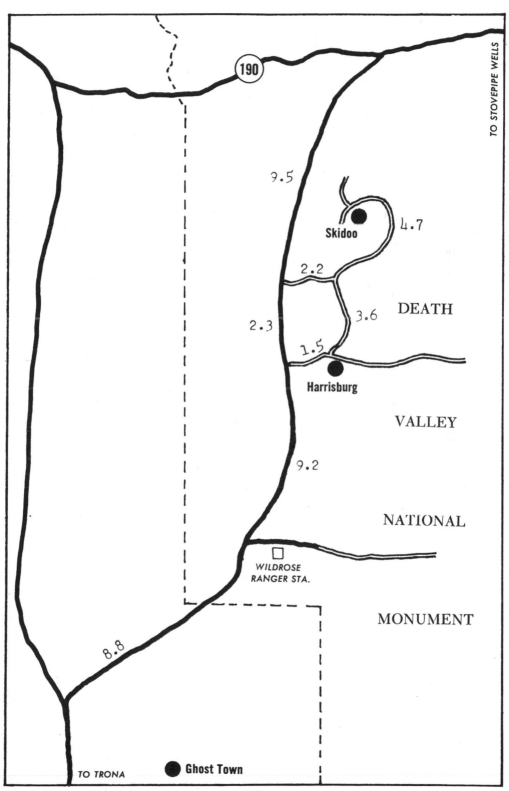

190

TO STOVEPIPE WELLS

9.5

Skidoo

4.7

2.2

2.3

3.6

1.5

Harrisburg

DEATH

VALLEY

9.2

NATIONAL

WILDROSE
RANGER STA.

MONUMENT

8.8

TO TRONA

● Ghost Town

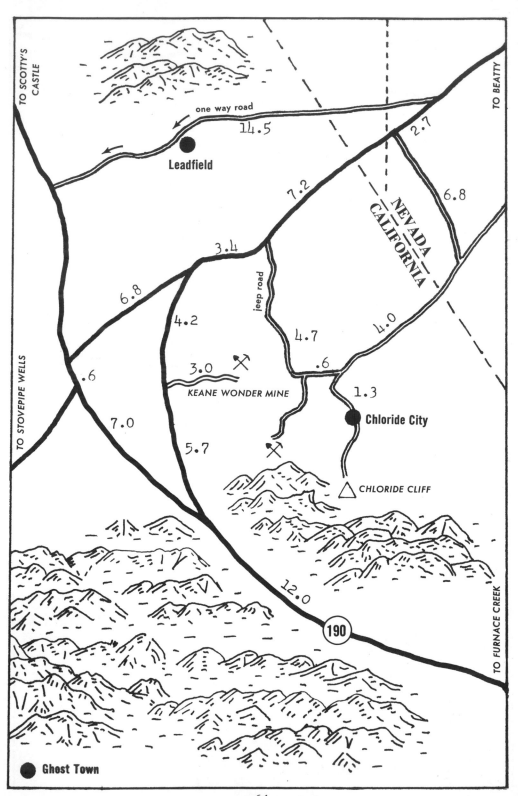

TO SCOTTY'S CASTLE

TO BEATTY

one way road

14.5

Leadfield

2.7

7.2

6.8

NEVADA
CALIFORNIA

3.4

6.8

jeep road

4.2

4.7

4.0

3.0

.6

KEANE WONDER MINE

1.3

TO STOVEPIPE WELLS

.6

Chloride City

7.0

5.7

△ CHLORIDE CLIFF

12.0

190

TO FURNACE CREEK

● Ghost Town

LEADFIELD — Located in beautiful Titus Canyon in Death Valley National Monument. Leadfield boomed in 1926 to a peak of 300 people. The post office operated only 8 months and the town folded when it was discovered that the supposedly rich ore deposits never existed. The spectacular towering walls and beauty of titus Canyon make this trip worthwhile.

CHLORIDE CITY — Located in a remote corner of Death Valley National Monument at the northern end of the Funeral Mountain Range. Unlike the barren sites of Harrisburg and Skiddo, Chloride City has a few old buildings left, but these are fast falling victim to the elements. Several old mines are scattered through the hills. This is not a place to visit in the summer months, as the temperature soars well over 100 degrees.

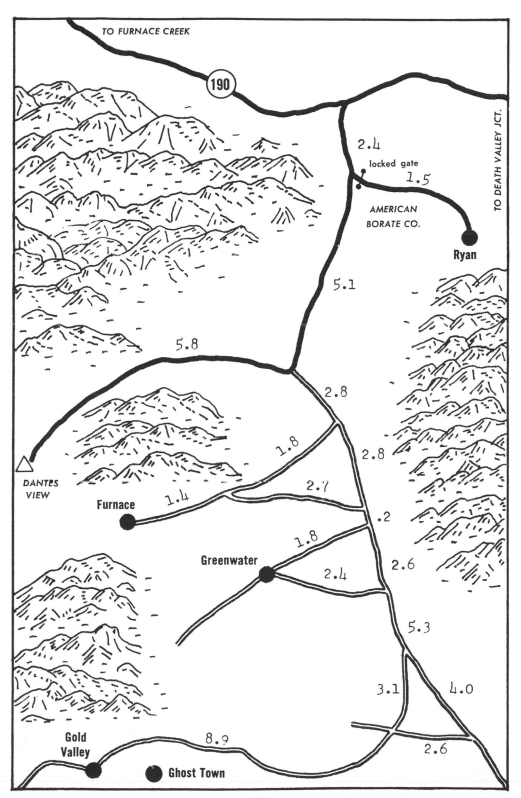

TO FURNACE CREEK

190

TO DEATH VALLEY JCT.

2.4

locked gate

1.5

AMERICAN
BORATE CO.

Ryan

5.1

5.8

2.8

1.8

2.8

.2

2.7

DANTES
VIEW

1.4

Furnace

1.8

Greenwater

2.4

2.6

5.3

3.1

4.0

Gold
Valley

8.9

2.6

Ghost Town

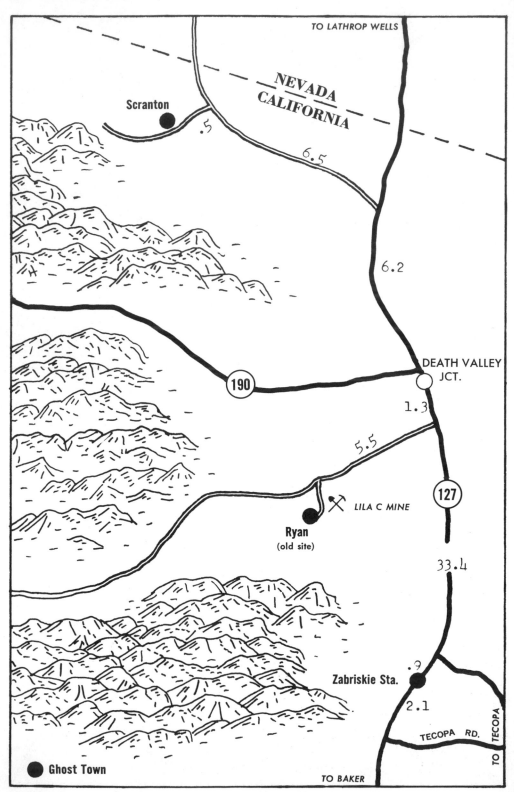

TO LATHROP WELLS

NEVADA
CALIFORNIA

Scranton

.5

6.5

6.2

190

DEATH VALLEY
JCT.

1.3

5.5

127

LILA C MINE

Ryan
(old site)

33.4

Zabriskie Sta.

.9

2.1

TECOPA RD.

TO TECOPA

● Ghost Town

TO BAKER

Chapter 5

The BLM Desert Country

As far as federal recreational lands are concerned, the recognizable property under the supervision of the Bureau of Land Management (BLM) bloomed late.

The author can remember accidentally bumping into the first so marked BLM campground he had ever seen up on the edge of the Kern Plateau at the southern end of the Sierra Nevada years after he knew about Sierran campgrounds administered by the Parks Department, the Forest Service, the State Division of Forestry and even Tulare County.

He had always considered that there were the National Parks, the National Forests, some military property and as far as government land was concerned, the BLM ran everything else, but he had never bumped into a BLM ranger or BLM naturalist, so he calculated they ran a pretty casual ship.

All that changed here in California with the BLM's highly visible involvement with that part of the California desert they administered. Outside of Death Valley National Monument, and Joshua Tree National Monument, outside Anza-Borrego Desert State Park, outside of the Naval Weapons Center (then the Naval Ordnance Test Station), outside the Naval aerial gunnery range in the Chocolate Mountains, outside the Marine Training Center at Twentynine Palms, outside the Naval Impact Area inside Anza-Borrego Desert State Park, a ghost town buff felt that so long as he was not driving into plainly posted private land, he could go anywhere.

The BLM Desert Plan, years in creation, changed a lot of that. Now there are many places in the BLM desert country where you can enter only on foot.

The BLM's conservatorship of much of the California Mojave and Colorado Desert Plan did not completely satisfy everyone. The hardnosed preservationists thought it was too arbitrary, didn't face all the worrisome environmental problems at hand. The off-roaders, the motorcycle racers, the ATV community, the "leave-it-alone-at-any-cost" folks were unhappy. There is ample evidence that vandals, from whatever persuasion, have been on hand and active in the desert for as far back as pretty girl calendars have hung on the walls of desert roadside auto repair and flat tire establishments.

Fires, bottle diggings, the hauling away of weathered "barn wood"

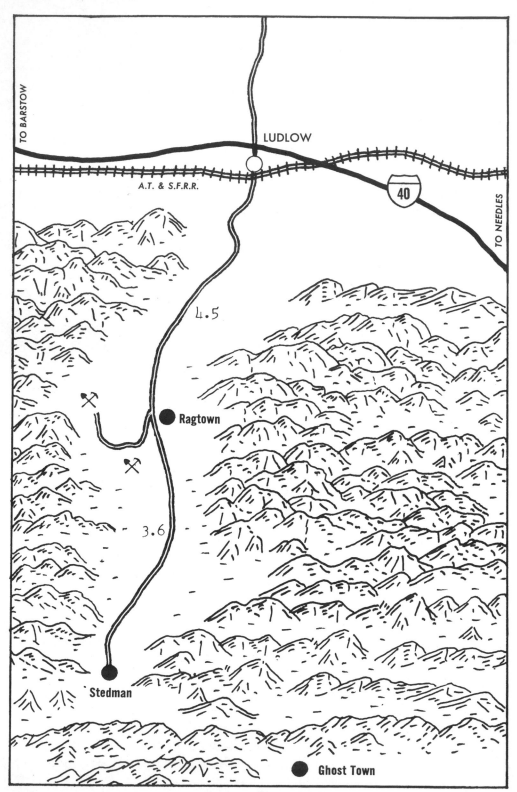

TO BARSTOW

LUDLOW

A.T. & S.F.R.R.

40

TO NEEDLES

4.5

Ragtown

3.6

Stedman

Ghost Town

or bits of old-timey wooden "gingerbread" took place. Some vandals just seemed to get rural pleasure from breaking things up.

The finest example of an eight-hole ghost town privy was there one visit, and a couple of years later it looked as if someone with a sledge hammer had let off steam banging its historic walls apart. My God, an eight-holer! Never saw anything in all our years of exploring to equal it!.

So it is entirely fitting and proper today to consider much of the desert country in California from around Death Valley south to the Yuma Country as the BLM Desert. Yes, there are islands that belong to other agencies. Joshua Tree, Anza-Borrego and the military inholding are foremost. But, many of the worthwhile old desert camps are carefully looked after by the BLM rangers.

For reasons that need not be dwelt upon, the BLM rangers carry sidearms today. In the old days it was never thought necessary. But even so, they remain wise and thoughtful protectors of what they patrol. And just because you don't see them, don't get the notion that they don't see you.

The BLM outlines the history of the California desert in these terms:

Early travelers through the Mojave Desert included the Piute, Chemehuevi, and Mojave Indian tribes. Although there was probably a network of trails leading from the Colorado River to the Mojave River Sink near Soda Springs, two main routes of travel apparently were used. One ran through Foshay Pass to Kelso Dunes and on to Soda Lake. The other route, which apparently was more heavily used, lay farther north and passed from Piute Creek to Soda Spring. This Indian trail evolved into a pack trail and later into the wagon road that became known as the Mojave Road, Mojave Trail or Old Government Road. The Mojave Road became very important to California and to the nation. It was the major route serving California, Nevada and Arizona until the Santa Fe Railroad was built in the early 1800's across the desert from San Francisco to Needles.

Many well-traveled Indian routes served as precursers not only to wagon roads, but also to postal routes and eventually to railroads such as the Union Pacific.

Promoters of the transcontinental railroad were sensitive to the fact that the only enterprise along the empty miles of the California desert was mining, and the railroad made every effort to accommodate the prospectors. During these "Great Years" (1900-1919), more mines were opened and operated profitably than in any

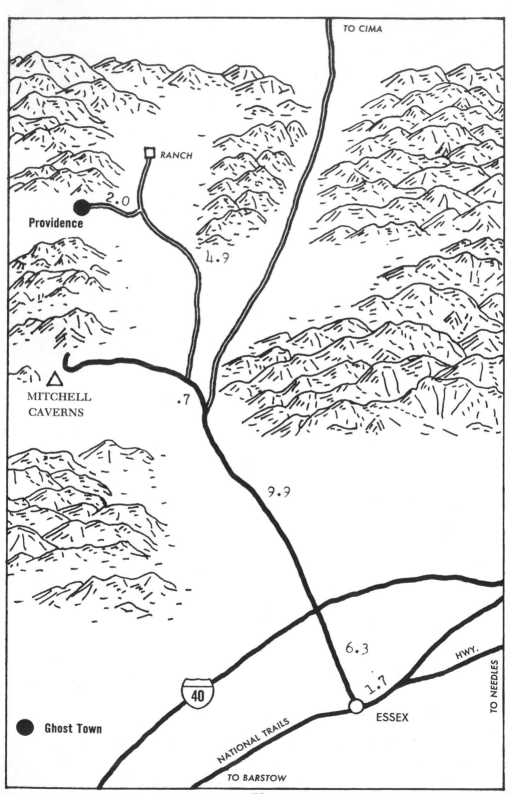

TO CIMA

RANCH

2.0

Providence

4.9

MITCHELL
CAVERNS

.7

9.9

6.3

40

1.7

HWY.

TO NEEDLES

ESSEX

● Ghost Town

NATIONAL TRAILS

TO BARSTOW

PROVIDENCE — A silver mining town of the 1880's, located about 3 miles north of Mitchell Caverns in the Providence Mountains. The principal mine that supported the camp was The Bonanza King. Several building frames, walls, dugouts, and foundations remain today. The elevation here is about 4,000 feet, but it still gets mighty hot in the summer months, and nights are cold during the winter months.

other period in San Bernardino County history. The mining boom created numerous towns, now almost all ghosted, in the Mojave Desert, including Vanderbilt, Providence, and Hart. Cima, Goffs, Kelso, Fenner, Essex, Ivanpah II and III also owe their creation to mining and the railroads.

Settlers driving their wagons over the Mojave Road grazed their animals on the plentiful grasses they found across the rich rangelands

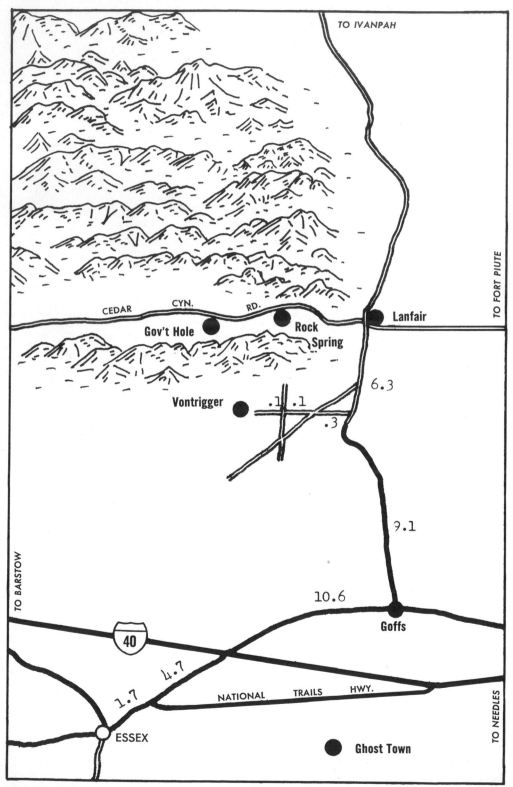

TO IVANPAH

TO FORT PIUTE

CEDAR   CYN.   RD.

Gov't Hole   Rock
              Spring

Lanfair

6.3

Vontrigger   .1 .1

.3

9.1

TO BARSTOW

10.6

40

Goffs

4.7

1.7

NATIONAL   TRAILS   HWY.

TO NEEDLES

ESSEX

Ghost Town

LANFAIR — Now in complete ruins, only a couple of walls and foundations remain among the Joshua Trees that abound in this area. Lanfair was once quite a good sized town that spread over a large area, but it is difficult now to detect where most of the buildings stood.

of the Cima Dome and Lanfair Valley country. Immense herds of sheep and cattle were driven over the Mojave Road to Arizona and on into New Mexico.

The first cattle ranching business in the East Mojave area began in the late 1800's. In 1894, the Rock Spring Land and Cattle Company was incorporated and became a dominant force, extending their operations throughout most of the eastern Mojave and a large chunk of southern Nevada. The Ox Cattle Company remains today as a direct descendant of the Rock Spring Land and Cattle Company.

The Mojave Desert retains intriguing and colorful names linked closely with the past. You may want to visit such places as Lanfair, Goffs, Kelso, Rock Spring, Hole-in-the-Wall, and Fort Piute.

In regard to off-road vehicle (ORV) use, all public lands in the California desert are designated in one of three vehicle-use categories: "Open," "Closed," or "Limited."

"Open Areas" are those available for cross-country use. Vehicles may be operated anywhere within the posted boundaries of these areas.

"Closed Areas" are closed to all vehicles including off-road types. Hiking, horseback riding, and other forms of nonvehicular use are permitted.

"Limited Areas" are those where vehicles use is allowed subject to some restrictions. In some limited areas, use is permitted on existing routes, but cross-country travel is not allowed. In other limited areas, use is limited to specific "approved routes." Some areas may also be limited with respect to the time of year vehicles may be operated there or the types of vehicles that may be used. Limited use restrictions are specified on the signs marking the boundaries of the areas or on maps available from BLM offices. Unless otherwise posted, wayside parking or camping is limited to within 300 feet of routes of travel in limited areas.

The vast open spaces of the California Desert are uniquely situated within a few hours' drive of over 12 million people. In recognition of the special challenges created by this situation, Congress established the California Desert Conservation Area (CDCA) in 1976. Approximately half of the desert's 25 million acres are public lands administered by the BLM, an agency of the U.S. Department of the Interior.

Congress directed the BLM to provide for the administration of public lands in the CDCA in a way that would protect its unusual natural and cultural values while providing for the wise use of its resources. The administrative headquarters for the CDCA are located at the BLM's California Desert District Office in Riverside. Public lands are managed for a variety of uses, including minerals, livestock grazing, wildlife, watershed, wilderness, and recreation.

The address of the California Desert District Office is 1695 Spruce Street, Riverside, California 92507, (714) 351-6394.

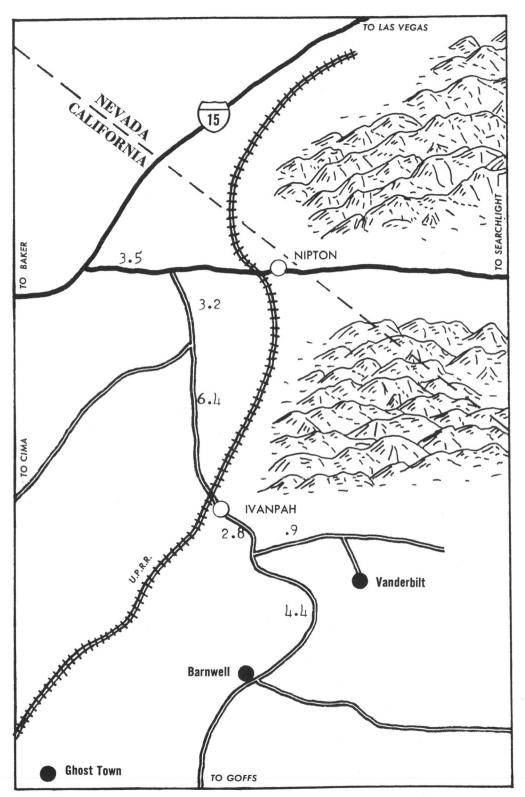

TO LAS VEGAS

NEVADA
CALIFORNIA

15

TO BAKER

TO SEARCHLIGHT

3.5

NIPTON

3.2

6.4

TO CIMA

IVANPAH

2.8

.9

U.P.R.R.

Vanderbilt

4.4

Barnwell

Ghost Town

TO GOFFS

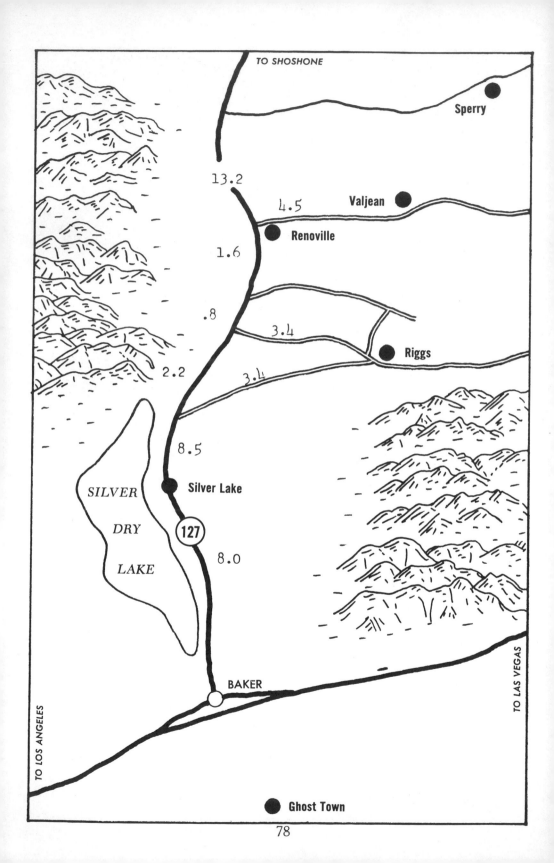

SILVER LAKE — *An old railroad town located on the old Tonopah and Tidewater Railroad. This railroad was abandoned long ago and the tracks were torn out for salvage. Most of the buildings have collapsed now and just a few foundations remain. Other towns along the Tonopah and Tidewater include Riggs, Valjean, and Sperry, but these sites are now barren of buildings.*

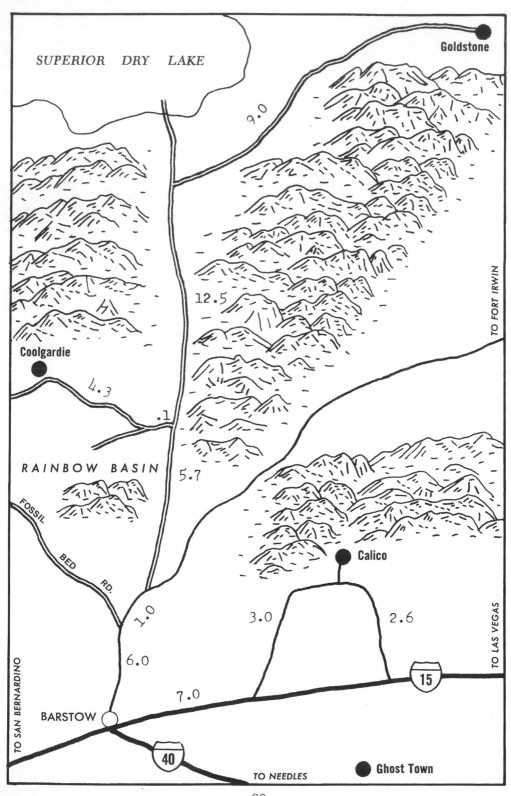

SUPERIOR DRY LAKE

Goldstone

9.0

TO FORT IRWIN

12.5

Coolgardie

4.3

.1

RAINBOW BASIN

5.7

FOSSIL

BED

RD.

Calico

1.0

3.0

2.6

TO LAS VEGAS

6.0

TO SAN BERNARDINO

7.0

BARSTOW

15

40

TO NEEDLES

Ghost Town

CALICO — This town developed in 1881 from silver discoveries in the Calico Mountains. The silver deposits were fabulously rich and produced $16 to $20 million dollars in silver ore and borates before the price of silver dropped in 1896 and the town became a ghost. A few years ago Walter Knott, of Knott's Berry Farm, restored the town as closely as possible to the original, making it an interesting and exciting place to visit. In 1966 the Knott family deeded their holdings to San Bernardino County, and it is now managed by the Regional Parks Department.

GOLDSTONE — Gold was first discovered in this area around 1850. It was several years later before the town of Goldstone was settled, and she has known many booms since then, the latest being 1920. For many years NASA has had extensive installations here, marked by large space antennaes.

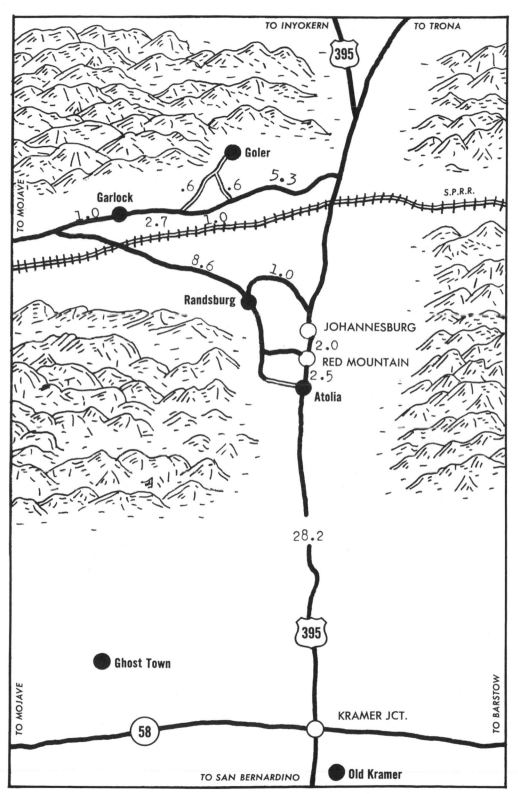

TO INYOKERN

TO TRONA

395

Goler

.6 .6 5.3

S.P.R.R.

Garlock

TO MOJAVE

1.0 2.7 1.0

8.6 1.0

Randsburg

JOHANNESBURG

2.0

RED MOUNTAIN

2.5

Atolia

28.2

395

Ghost Town

TO MOJAVE

TO BARSTOW

KRAMER JCT.

58

TO SAN BERNARDINO

Old Kramer

GARLOCK — Originally called Cow Wells.
  This little town flourished in 1896. The gold ore from the Yellow Aster Mine at nearby Randsburg was hauled down the hill to the stamp mill at Garlock. A few wooden buildings remain standing today, along with many sunken foundations to mark the site of a once busy and important little town.

RANDSBURG — The Yellow Aster Mine was discovered in 1895 and the town of Randsburg and surrounding area boomed to around 4,000 people. The district eventually produced $60 million in gold. The town had her first big fire in December of 1897. The fire was soon extinguished, but about a month later another conflagration wiped out half of the camp. A short while later, still another fire wiped out the other half.

In later years nearby discoveries of silver and tungsten revived the area but it has never grown very large since the first boom. Many of the old buildings remain today and the area abounds with old mine dumps. There is a fine museum at Randsburg.

PATTON'S SHRINE — *In the Iron Mountains of the Mojave Desert stands this stone shrine built by GIs while on desert maneuvers under General George Patton prior to the US invasion of North Africa during World War Two. There are many traces of Patton's desert army and of the later "Desert Strike" maneuvers in this part of the desert.*

Chapter 6

Joshua Tree
National Monument Country

While there are several National Monuments in California, two of them are principally large regions of the California desert.

The first, and perhaps the better known, is Death Valley National Monument.

The second is Joshua Tree National Monument, lying within Riverside and San Bernardino counties, and nominally set aside because it is the principal habitat of the Joshua Tree, a plant form in the cactus family, which holds its supplicating arms aloft.

While the western desert of California and Mexico holds a rather sizeable list of strange, rare, large desert plants, the Southwest lays claim to two major species — the Joshua Tree and the Saguaro. There is probably no place in the geography of the Southwest where the two grow side by side, but there is a visual similarity. Joshua Tree: Southern California; Saguaro: Arizona and Northern Mexico. Many motion pictures have been filmed showing the U.S. Cavalry fighting the Arizona Apaches or the Yaqui Indians of Sonora, Mexico, surrounded by Joshua Trees (which are native to Southern California). Likewise there are Southern California desert films shot among the similar but decidedly different Saguaro.

Perhaps someone who is a detailed and observant traveler can think of a site somewhere in the Colorado River Country where the two plants, the Joshua Tree and the Saguaro, live side by side.

Of course, Joshua Tree National Monument was not set aside as a National Monument simply because of the Joshua Trees. There are other attractions, many other exotic cacti, vast areas of megalithic boulders, some of them fashioned into natural arches. At one time this area was noted for a certain kind of diminutive barrel cactus. This was before the "cactus garden" craze hit Southern California sometime prior to World War Two. Now vast tracts of the desert country once porcupined with small barrel cacti sit picked clean. The giant boulders

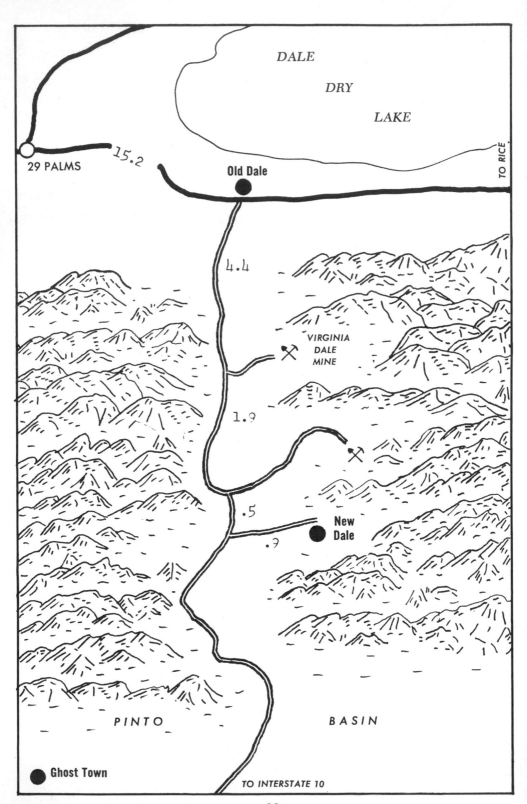

DALE DRY LAKE

29 PALMS   15.2   Old Dale

TO RICE

4.4

VIRGINIA DALE MINE

1.9

.5

New Dale

.9

PINTO   BASIN

Ghost Town

TO INTERSTATE 10

within the Monument are often used by both tyro and experienced rock climbers.

While the country is rich in archaeological sites, within the Monument is the famous Pinto Basin where a particular family of aboriginal man lived and flourished. He fashioned a specialized arrow point that is known, naturally, as the Pinto Point. The region touches on the ancient savannah country that existed in this portion of the Great Basin after the recession of the last Ice Age, and in remote caves remnants of ground sloth have been found. Not far away, in a small, hidden cave, have been found, still brightly painted, sections of the very primitive — pre-bow-and-arrow — atlatl, the spear throwing device.

Naturally there was vast mineralization in this area and mines sprang up in the region, both inside and outside the Monument. Just to the east are the famous Three Dale mines, the Supply Mine and a string of others. This area outside the monument is best explored with an off-road vehicle.

Inside the Monument are the equally famous, or — considering the tales of banditry and bloodshed connected with them — equally infamous mines, the Desert Queen and the Lost Horse Mine. Both can be found by following Monument maps and signs.

Rick Anderson, current Superintendent of Joshua Tree National Monument, wrote the following words about his feeling toward the ghost camps in the area he oversees, and the ghost camps throughout this state:

"The ghost towns and old mining districts that I have visited in California are certainly fascinating. Fortunately, there is a good deal of history available on some of them. As I look at the old structures, millsites, tunnels, and shafts, I can't help but realize that those old-timers who did the work were pretty tough customers. Lumber supplies and equipment in many cases had to be hauled for miles and miles, and by horse and wagon. The same is true in some cases for firewood for cooking and heating water, which is certainly the case with some of the ghost towns within and adjacent to Joshua Tree National Monument.

"Moreover, in these areas simply getting a drink of water is often a chore, for water sources in this area are few and far between.

"It is a shame that so many of these structures that are part of our heritage have been so badly vandalized over the years. They have such a place in our history, that generations to come should have the chance to view them as they exist today. Unfortunately there is an element of our society that is totally irresponsible with regard to the rights of others."

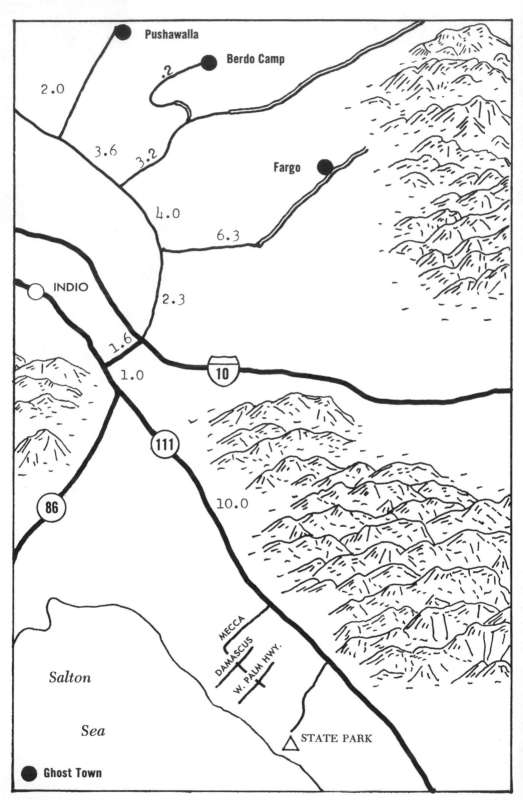

Pushawalla

Berdo Camp

.2

2.0

3.6

3.2

Fargo

4.0

6.3

2.3

INDIO

1.6

1.0

10

111

10.0

86

MECCA

DAMASCUS

W. PALM HWY.

Salton

Sea

△ STATE PARK

● Ghost Town

BERDOO CAMP — Newer than most ghost towns, Berdoo Camp was built in the early 1930's when the Metropolitan Water District was constructing the Colorado River Aqueduct. The District put up the town and rented the buildings to the men and their families who worked on the aqueduct. Several other camps were built along the aqueduct but none as large as Berdoo Camp.

The Coachella section of the aqueduct was completed in 1937 and the camp was abandoned. Many walls and foundations remain today as mute evidence of the tremendous job done here.

Hume Mill

Hume Mill

Chapter 7

The Sierra Nevada

While the Mother Lode Country is encompassed within the largest range of mountains in the "lower 48," there are other spectacular ghost camps in those high mountains that have little or nothing at all to do with the Gold Rush.

When the sequoia gigantia (the big redwoods of the Sierra) were first discovered in 1858, lumbermen rejoiced almost as much as the

Photo By
J. H. Traver

HUME — *This is located in an area of the Sequoia Kings Canyon National Park region that was heavily logged for the giant redwoods. Lumber from this mill was flumed down the west side of the Sierra Nevada to the San Joaquin Valley community of Sanger. Only the old dam at Hume reminds visitors of the boom logging days.*

prospectors who found rich gold lodes in the Sierran foothills. A few lumbermen got rich on redwood.

Getting timber claims in the new state seemed to present little problem to the determined loggers who found that redwood was an incredible wood. It was resistant to almost all rot or decay. Resistant even to some insects, it could be used as foundation timbers and last for years. Redwood was a "miracle" lumber of its day . . . and it came in such incredibly large packages. Trees were more than 20 feet in diameter and 200 feet high.

Alas, there had to be drawbacks. The giant redwoods were difficult to fell. It was hard to cut down a tree with a 30-foot long two-man hand-pulled crosscut saw. Axe work took forever. The trees had the habit of shattering on crashing to the earth. Loggers learned to fashion beds

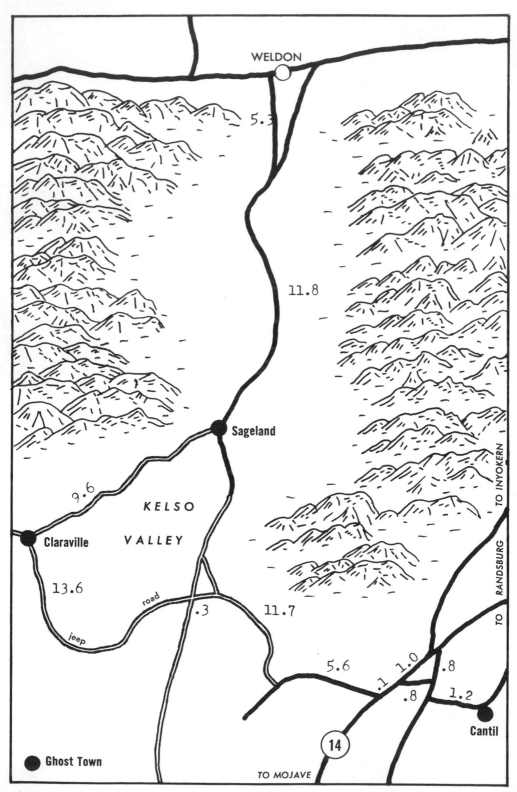

WELDON

5.3

11.8

Sageland

9.6

KELSO

VALLEY

Claraville

13.6

road

.3

11.7

jeep

5.6

.1 1.0 .8

.8 1.2

TO INYOKERN

TO RANDSBURG

Cantil

14

● Ghost Town

TO MOJAVE

CLARAVILLE — All the old buildings at this once busy mining community high in the Piute Mountains of Kern County have been moved or torn down. This old courthouse, made with square nails and wooden pegs now stands in Pioneer Village in Bakersfield. But there are other mining relics in the remote Piutes.

of boughs from lesser trees to try to ease the fall of the towering, enormous-girthed sequoias.

Getting to the individual stands of sequoia gigantia, which grew at elevations as high as 8000 feet, was difficult. Roads had to be built by hand.

And then getting the sawn redwood "down the hill" was even more of a challenge. In some places long flumes were built in the Sierra. One, from Hume Lake (now within Sequoia Kings Canyon National

Park) down to the San Joaquin Valley flatland community of Sanger, was an engineering marvel. (For those who know the precise route of the old flume line, it is possible to hike in and still see bits and pieces of the 59-mile ruin.)

There are lovely anecdotes of loggers riding on "boats" or "rafts" down the flume to enjoy a night on the town in Sanger. Anecdotes tell of injured folks from the logging camps going down the flume for first aid. One story even tells of a pregnant woman who rode down the flume so that she could have proper medical attention.

After the hand-built wooden flumes came the logging railroads. Fascinating volumes have been written about these lines, mostly narrow-gauge, often using special little Shay engines designed for difficult mountain work. There are records of mountain railroads, designed to haul logs and lumber from the Northern Sierra as far south as the San Bernardino Mountains in the San Bernardino National Forest. Other logging railroads made incredible runs in the Yosemite and Hetch Hetchy Country. Some logging railroads pierced the Sierra from the eastern side, into the slopes north of Truckee.

The ghost towns in this chapter then are principally logging camps that boomed and vanished. In Converse Basin, where the town of Millwood was situated, greedy loggers took out every single loggable giant in the basin, save one. Conscience touched even them for a foreman insisted they leave behind one giant, the Boole Tree, 269 feet tall, which explorers into the Millwood site can still visit.

To the east the Hume Basin was similarly logged almost bare. A dam was built here in 1908 to supply the Hume with water. A mill town boomed.

There are two kinds of native sequoias in California: The Sequoia gigantea, the Big Tree, the redwood of the Sierra Nevada; and the Sequoia sempervirens, the Coast redwoods which grow in many of California's northern coastal counties.

When cut, the Coast redwood will come up again from the stumpage. It is a replenishable redwood tree. The gigantia does not have this characteristic. There is some seedling reproduction in the area where the giants were cut — the sequoia has the smallest cone of the conifers — but those seeds grow slowly. No one, in a lifetime, will see a Sierra redwood grow from a seedling to forest giant.

In time, redwood logging in the Sierra ended. it was cheaper to log along the Coast. Preservationists were having their say — Coast redwoods would come back quickly; gigantia could not.

Millwood and Hume and other such mill towns in probably what is

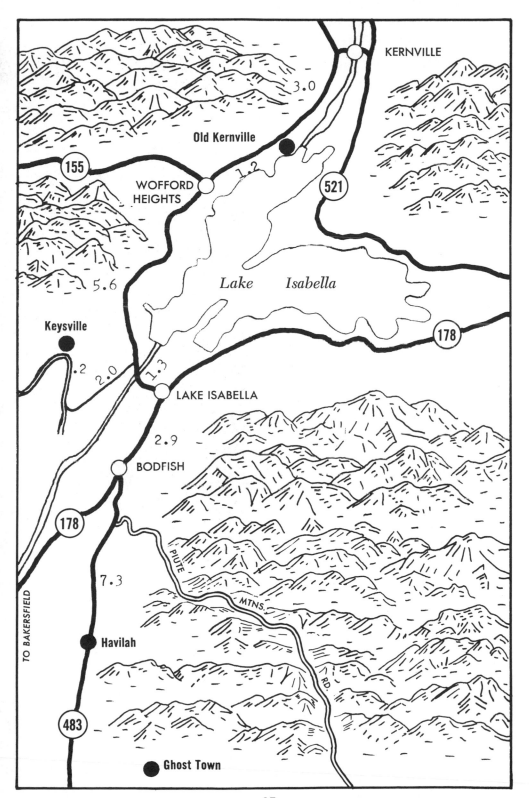

KERNVILLE

3.0

Old Kernville

155

521

WOFFORD
HEIGHTS

1.2

Lake   Isabella

5.6

178

Keysville

.2   2.0   1.3

LAKE ISABELLA

2.9

BODFISH

178

PIUTE

MTNS.

7.3

TO BAKERSFIELD

RD.

Havilah

483

Ghost Town

ATWOOD MILL — The explorer on foot in the deep woods near Mineral King in Sequoia-Kings Canyon National Park can come across relics of this old redwood logging center. Nearby is another old camp: Silver City. And not far away is the magnificent bowl of Mineral King itself — the town here was destroyed by avalanches again and again, winter after winter.

some of the most spectacularly beautiful and appealing country in the West ghosted. The railroads ceased operation; only in a few places can you find ties or even the old roadbeds.

Places like Millwood and Hume were cold and rough in the winter, but in the rest of the year they came about as close to Shangri-La as a Californian will ever know.

The Converse Basin and Hume sites have been logged, so have Balch Park and Mountain Home. But there are many of the Sierra Big Trees left — dozens of groves of them that run south from the Calaveras Big Trees to an almost hidden grove off the Western Divide Highway near the Forest Service station of Double Bunk, up from California Hot Springs in Kern County. There are Big Trees on the road into Mineral King and into Clough Cave. All are protected.

Here and there among them you can still find the marks of the logging ghost camps. And you must envy the men and women and children who lived in these aromatic, splendid places pushed up against the sky.

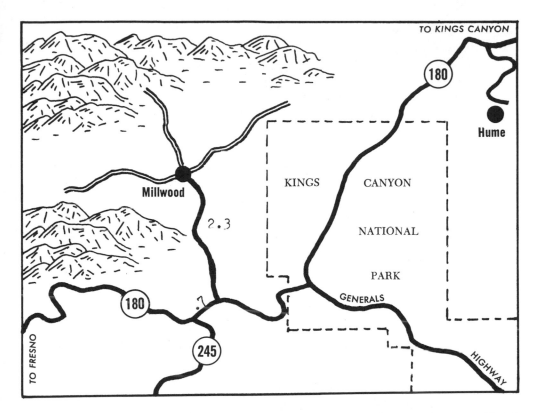

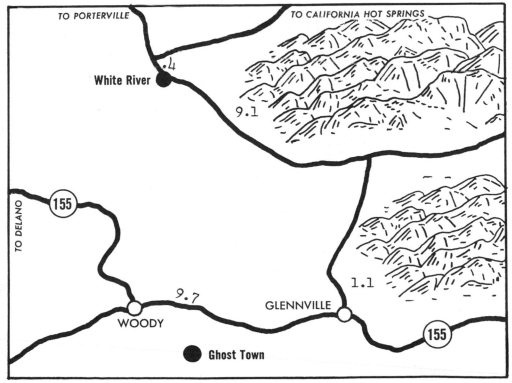

MILLWOOD — This is the Boole Tree, one of the largest sequoia gigantea to stand in Converse Basin after that enormous grove of giant redwoods was logged. It was the decision of the logging boss that at least one single tree be spared here, and he picked this giant. The Boole Tree is still there, on view. Millwood, the camp, has vanished.

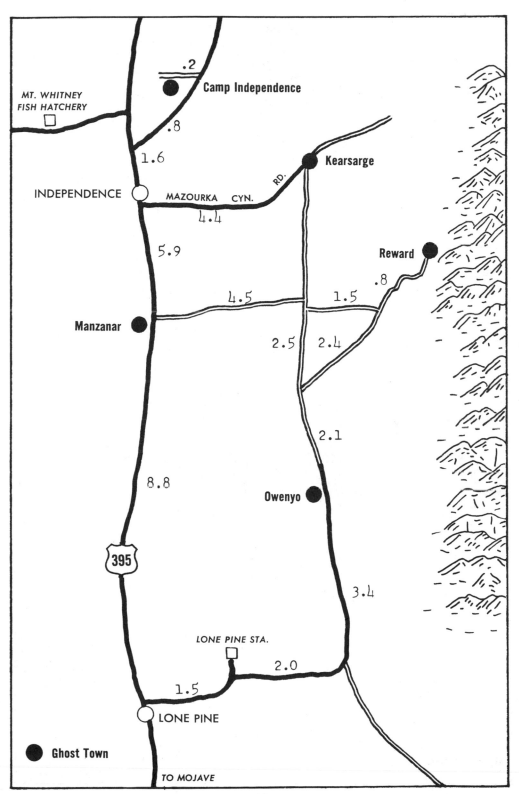

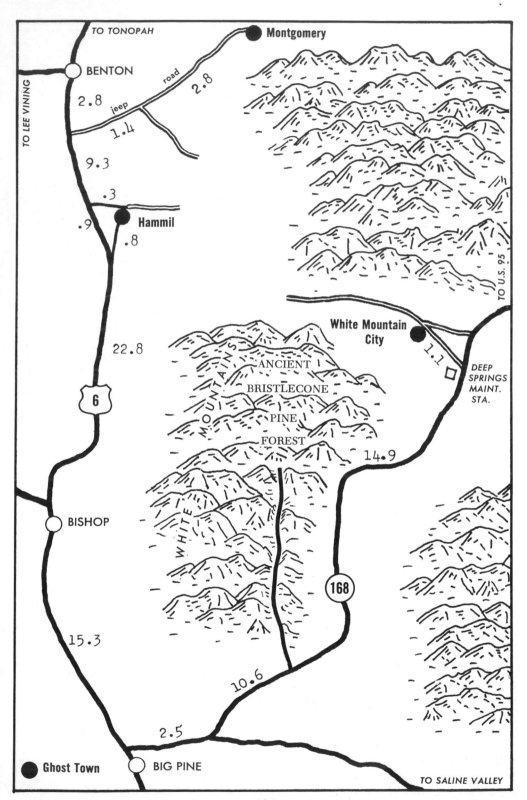

TO TONOPAH

Montgomery

BENTON

2.8

jeep road 2.8

1.4

9.3

.3

.9 Hammil

.8

TO LEE VINING

22.8

6

White Mountain City

1.1

TO U.S. 95

DEEP SPRINGS MAINT. STA.

ANCIENT BRISTLECONE PINE FOREST

WHITE MOUNTAINS

14.9

168

BISHOP

15.3

10.6

2.5

Ghost Town   BIG PINE

TO SALINE VALLEY

Chapter 8

Along the Coast

If it is the tale of the vanished gold town that excites you, write down the name of Klamath City. Built in 1851 at the mouth of the Klamath River in Del Norte County, it was platted to be a port of entry into the gold-rich, inaccessible back country. After all, weren't the mysterious Klamath and Smith and Trinity rivers "back in there somewhere" all asparkle with placer gold?

But Klamath City suffered from wave and storm, shifting sandbars and a decidedly undecided river mouth (it never seemed to be sure just where it wanted to be). A year later the town was deserted.

Even with a crystal ball you could probably not find the site of old Klamath City today, but take some small heart in the fact that the Klamath River mouth still hates to be nailed down; still moody and undecided. This river floods from time to time, and when it does, the present day towns of Klamath and Requa catch hob. You can find the buttress of an old bridge on the lower Klamath on the ocean side, decorated with statues of a big old bear. The old bridge is gone, but even on its most placid days you can be sure that the Klamath River down below is still sluicing grains of wheat gold out to sea, a dessert spoonful at a time. At nearby Gold Bluff miners once panned placer gold from the dark beach sands.

The back-country excitement left marks on the land here, if you can find the maps, or the people who remember . . . Make strong medicine before you go looking and then keep an eye peeled for the likes of these vanished, mostly forgotten camps in Del Norte County, not far from the line south where Jedediah Strong Smith first crossed over from Oregon territory into "California," and that was in 1828. This was wild, primitive country when Smith went through; he, a mountain man, a trapper, a trailblazer. Not many of his kind came this way.

So mark these lonesome sites where miners dug and prayed and some of them . . . Ah, but you know how it went:

Democratic Gulch, Butch Gulch, Jump-Off-Joe-Creek, House Creek, Hungry Hill, Galiceburg, Lucky Green, Wilderville, Quartzville, Coyote Creek, Murphy's Creek, Williamsburg, Webfoot

Mine, Slate Creek, Canyon Creek, Yankee-Doodle Mine. Smell like gold country?

Move up the Coast.

For a while Crescent City was the big town along the coast. It was for many years the chief port of entry into the remote mining excitement inland along the Siskiyou, the Trinity and other watercourses.

Crescent City grew. For years it resembled an elaborate motion picture set of the town that some historian might have recorded.

Move down the coast from Crescent City.

Mendocino County. Old logging camps, abandoned, old bleached silvered wooden fences, barns, outhouses and faded signs; — wooden everything, because wood was the cheapest thing there was. If one could learn to eat wood, folks in Mendocino County would have been the best fed in all the world.

But, times have changed. It seems that Mendocino County is still just as beautiful, just as green, just as able to give birth to new trees and berry patches, to support deer and bear.

However, for several years now Mendocino County has had a new industry — and even the old timers who live there, the shopkeepers in the small towns who used to make a living dealing with the logging folk, have differing opinions about what has happened.

A lot of marijuana is being grown in Mendocino. If you are inquisitive and poke around, you are a stranger and strangers are unwelcome.

The marijuana plantations pose more than a law enforcement problem. Possibly, if it was not for these illegal farms, some of the businesses that thrive now would go "bust." The logging industry in Mendocino is at rock bottom.

This is not a book about marijuana. It's about ghost towns. So, unless you have friends in this area, both up and down the coast from Mendocino, folks who are known and who will escort you into the old camps, tread gently. Some of the marijuana plantations are mom and pop operations, large enough only to grow it and make a living. Some of the farms are said to be associated with organized crime.

In Monterey County, you still have similar problems in the back country behind the Big Sur, but there is one choice area to consider. The Los Burros Mining District and the now burned away mining camps of Mars, Manchester, Queen, King and Grizzly once bloomed here. Manchester became the principal "town" and until a recent fire, there were buildings to see. Now it is a sad charred sight, but still a vivid reminder of gold in the Big Sur.

San Luis Obispo County has a wide belt of quicksilver ore with a scattering of vast old mining camps that run roughly from behind Hearst's Castle southeast through the roadless back country over the Santa Lucias, to the extant town of Klau, near Lake Nacimiento.

If you drive up the single avenue here, San Simeon Creek Road, from Highway One (jumpoff at the San Simeon Creek State Park), and keep your eyes peeled when you are four or five miles up this surprisingly and utterly delightful canyon drive, you will see a towering steel chimney stack on the northern horizon about a half-mile uphill. This is part of the old Cambria mercury smelter. It is on private property and it was a major operation. Old topo maps show many diggings, a jeep track that reaches deep and high into the spectacular Santa Lucias, even a couple of old, old cemeteries (probably now on private land).

From Santa Barbara County south to San Diego County there is little more than some hard-to-find mission asistencias or camps that we have dealt with elsewhere.

Still, ghost camps, decaying old towns are everywhere in the state. Within sight of San Francisco is Angel Island, and on the far edge of the Bay is the old sailing ship port of Benecia. The magnificent old U.S. Armory is at Benecia. Each of the massive old quarried stone piles is in wonderful condition, and each is proudly dated in metal.

Chapter 9

Northern California

As mentioned previously, John Marshall's find in the millrace at Sutter's Mill in 1848 simply was not the initial discovery of gold in California. There was that discovery in Placerita Canyon, Los Angeles County, in 1843.

The records show that Indians had found gold in streams all over the northern parts of the state, but they had largely ignored it. The Spaniards whose gold fever had destroyed the Inca Empire in Peru, and who had done almost as much damage in their search for gold and silver in Mexico (and who had actually chased the phantom of the Silver Cities of Cibola — Eldorado — deep into Kansas) still looked for gold in California — but with little enthusiasm.

Mexican prospectors worked rich pockets of gold in Alta, California. Many "later strikes" can be traced back to the fact that the site "had been worked earlier by Mexican prospectors." One example of this is Cerro Gordo, a silver deposit well known to Mexican prospectors long before it became a new "American discovery."

Flakes and small nuggets had been spotted in many streams by the Spaniards who had tramped a great deal of California before the Anglos came to trap, look for farm land and "poke around." The Spaniards now were interested in building missions and saving souls.

Still, much of California prior to the early 1800's was pretty much terra incognito to white men of any stamp, let alone those who could recognize gold or silver sign if they saw it.

Much of the Northern California country was avoided because it was difficult to get into and because of hostile Indians. There was no particular reason to go into such a tangle unless you were one of those crazy "mountain men" who went into all manner of inhospitable places simply because, as they explained it, "My stick floated in that direction."

So it was that while gold HAD been found in what we think of as the Mother Lode and elsewhere prior to the business with Marshall and Sutter on the American in 1848, not much had been made of it. Particularly in Northern California.

But, after Marshall, and after the stampede started, knowledgeable men, and some as green as the grass they waded through that spring and summer of 1849, fanned out in all directions from the heart of the excitement, the Mother Lode, looking for signs.

And they found it.

In some places, like along the Trinity River, the Smith, and the Klamath, they found lots of gold. Farther north, it was more than just battling nature to get out the gold. There were mean, murderous Indians to contend with. The Pitt River Indians were among the most hostile.

While California would soon become a state, and the U.S. Army would have outposts there, few of the forts, camps, outposts, etc., helped the early miners.

Fandango Pass in Modoc County got its name because a party of emigrants heading for the rich farmland in Oregon Territory climbed the Warner Mountains and espied Oregon close at hand to the northwest. They celebrated on the ridge that night for they were within sight of the land they had come so far to settle. That night the local Indians attacked the party. Years later, hikers were still finding arrowheads imbedded in weathered, burned parts of emigrant

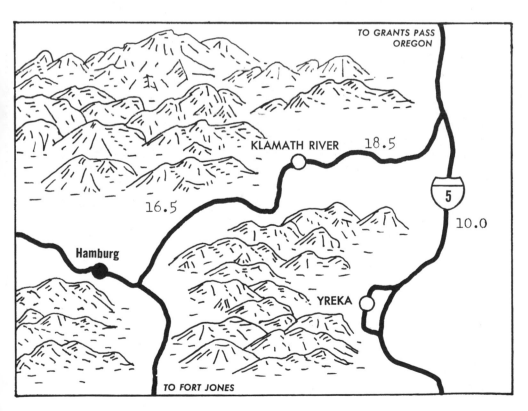

SHASTA — It was town-destroying fires that drove the settlers in the frontier camps like this one, remote Shasta, far west of the Mother Lode, to build their business houses of masonry. Often the window shutters were of heavy gauge iron to help suppress fires as well. Shasta's biggest disadvantage: It was terriby difficult to get to.

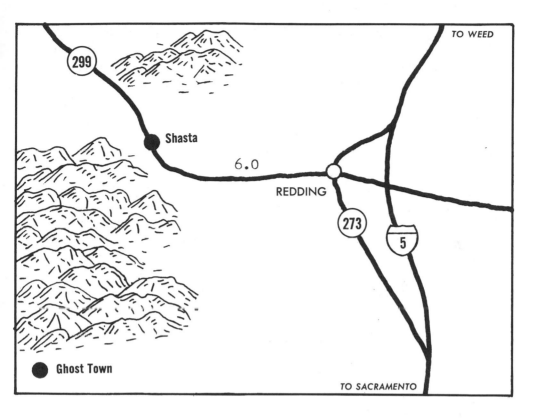

wagons there. Some years later Fort Bidwell would be situated nearby.

There are a number of old fort sites in the northern part of the state that ghost town enthusiasts should consider, both for the history and what, if anything, remains, and certainly for the gorgeous Northern California country.

Post offices were issued to Fort Bidwell, Fort Dick in Del Norte County, Fort Goff in Siskiyou County (not a military outpost), Fort Jones in Siskiyou County, Fort Seward in Humboldt County, and others.

Was it in Shasta or Trinity County where Major Pierson B. Reading first discovered gold at Reading's Bar in 1848? On the border, perhaps?

Another boom, another gold rush resulted here. A town, Shasta, was born in Shasta County but was a terribly hard place to get to from any direction. You could get just so close by the Sacramento River. Then it was all pack string and in those days the pack string folks were asking $1000 a ton for 188 miles along an old trail that just might have first been scratched out by some early Hudson Bay Company muleteers/fur trappers/explorers. (Fur trappers tramped most of California. "Not much count," they said. "No beaver.")

Shasta and the country around it were rich, and the town grew. The route into it was improved, but it was still tough slogging. Between 1852 and 1857 Shasta boasted a population of several thousand souls. Miners around the area could make $200 a day placering, and Shasta was calculated in 1857 to be the 15th largest city in the state.

In June of 1853 a sudden fire gutted the town. In just a tick over thirty minutes the entire business district burned.

In four years the town rebuilt, this time most of it masonry with steel shuttered windows. The folks to the east, in the Sierra, had already learned the trick. Some of the wooden Mother Lode camps burned to the ground more than once, but rebuilt and kept going.

Mining was still going on all across the area. Weaverville came up. French Gulch. New sandbars were being placered. Shasta, once THE PLACE, or at least along the route to THE PLACE, was finally bypassed. Overnight, almost, it ghosted. There are still some marvelous remains there. It is a State Historic Park.

Some old timers in the area, folks in the back country who grow hay, or run a dairy herd, or sell firewood, or who simply sit in the sun and tell stories to outlanders, nod and swear there is still "a lot of gold" in Northern California. Why not?

Add that square mile for square mile it is probably the least densely populated, beautiful part of the state, that it holds the fewest paved roads. There are bits and pieces of old diggings that backpackers stumble across once in a while which look hardly changed from the day when the last miner out ran dry of beans and bacon and moved on . . . more than a hundred years ago.

There are a few roads that crisscross this country, spiderwebbing around Modoc and Siskiyou, Del Norte, Humboldt, Trinity, Shasta and Lassen counties, the Trinity Alps, some fine rivers and lakes.

We can promise you marvelous old barns; usually friendly, gregarious folks; fresh air; green mountains; bits and pieces of ghost camps more-or-less hidden here and there, even a few fine museums and — well, you knew this all already — a big fat wedge of what we once simply called God's country.

You can still scuff around the dirt closeby Shasta and uncover charcoal. But you'll still have to go some to find any trace of that Old Hudson Bay Company mule trail where $1000 a ton pack strings used to haul provisions to prospectors from the end-of-river into the placering go-devils of almost vanished Shasta.

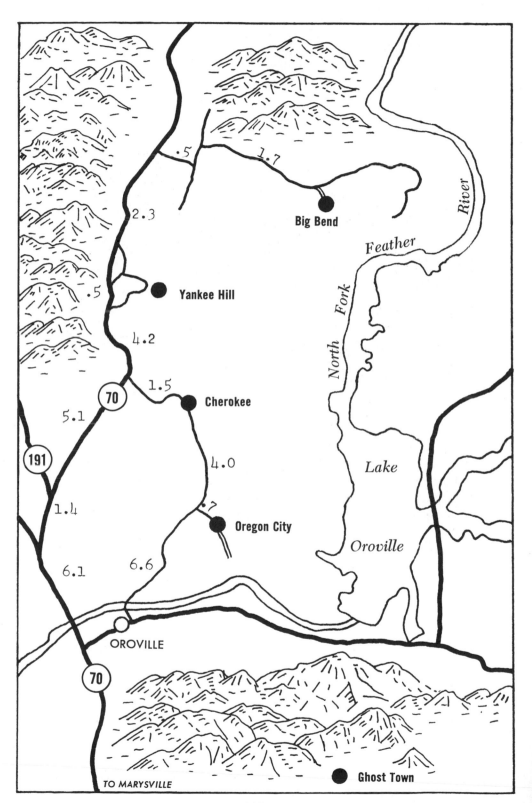

.5

1.7

2.3

Big Bend

Feather

River

North Fork

.5

Yankee Hill

4.2

1.5

70

Cherokee

5.1

4.0

191

Lake

.7

1.4

Oregon City

Oroville

6.1

6.6

OROVILLE

70

Ghost Town

TO MARYSVILLE

CHEROKEE — Gold was discovered here in 1850 by a band of Cherokee Indians. Mining commenced and a town was established in 1853, reaching her heyday in 1875 with a population of over 1,000 people.

Cherokee is the site of the world's greatest hydraulic gold mine, covering 26,000 acres, with 100 miles of sluice box. Over 300 men were employed day and night and the gold production exceeded $15 million.

The first diamonds in the United States were discovered here, the largest weighing 6 carats.

BIG BEND — Big Bend was a little community situated on the hill in the big bend of the North Fork of the Feather River. Since the town was abandoned, most of the old structures have collapsed. Every now and then someone will move into one of the remaining buildings and occupy it for a while, but most of the time the site is completely deserted.

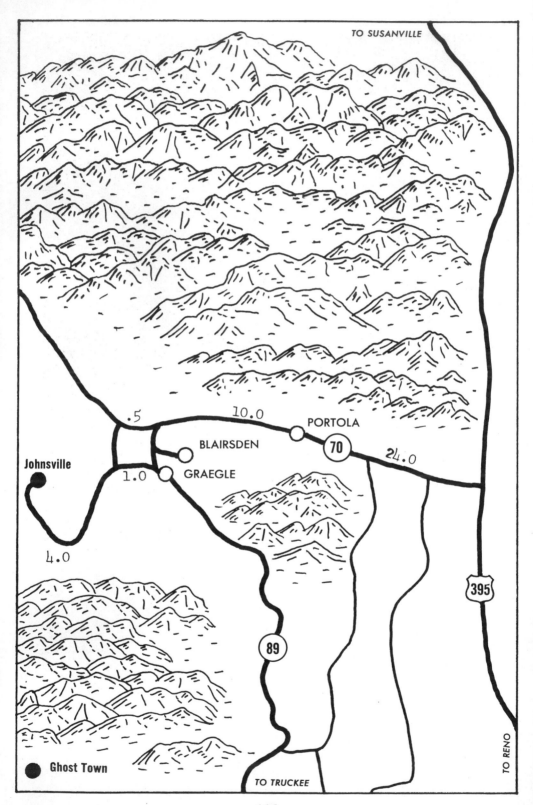

TO SUSANVILLE

.5   10.0   PORTOLA
BLAIRSDEN   70
Johnsville   1.0   GRAEGLE   24.0

4.0

89   395

Ghost Town

TO TRUCKEE   TO RENO

JOHNSVILLE — A slumbering old mining town that once knew a population of 7,000 people well over a century ago. The highly productive Plumas-Eureka Mine yielded many millions of dollars in gold and was the main support of the camp.

People are again moving into the ancient houses, but the town will never again regain her former status.

HAYDEN HILL — *An old gold mining camp perched on the side of a hill high in snow country. Gold was discovered in 1869 and the town of Hayden Hill was born. Winter snow and winds are hard on structures in this part of the country, so few buildings remain standing.*

Gold may still be found in the surrounding area, but it takes a lot of hardrock mining and milling to retrieve a small amount.

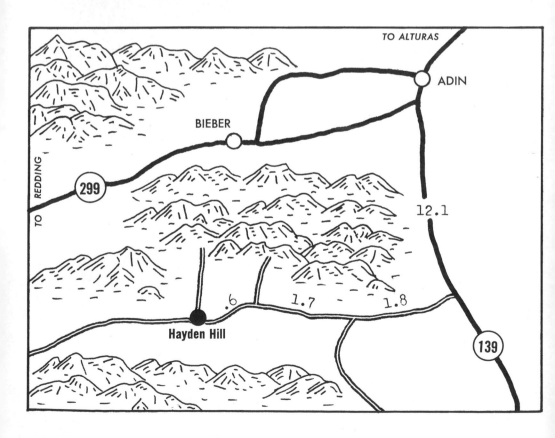

Chapter 10

Southern California

In the Coast Range, the Santa Lucias, up just a few miles from that marvelous ocean-hugging Highway One, there once existed a sizeable gold mining district. There was a town there, a regular town, complete with post office. It was called Mansfield and quite a lot of it existed as a ghost camp long after the mines had closed. The equipment that the metal thieves hadn't hauled away was still in place. Then the Los Padres National Forest suffered a terrible Coast Range fire and almost all of the wooden structures were burned.

You can still get there today, with Forest Service approval, best in an off-road vehicle. Some of the ruins are on private land.

Farther south, in San Luis Obispo County, quite lost, but once a town with schools and post office, was a quicksilver camp called Josephine. Finding it, or if you do think you might have figured out where it is, getting permission to visit the place since it is deep, deep away from any road on private property, is difficult. But it is back there in the hills, somewhere. Tantalizing.

In the same quicksilver belt, on private land and see-able only from a nearby road, is the boom mercury camp of Klau. And close to that, Adelaida. All are more or less ghosted, but with a few people still living nearby. It is lovely country.

On south, in Santa Barbara County now, is the vanished town of Asphaltea. This is another one of those marvelous camps in California not many have seen, nor does a photograph of it seem to exist. But it had a post office. It boomed because it exported tar, or possibly a crude oil. It, too, is deep in private property.

In Ventura County there were a number of booming gold camps in what is now the Chuchupate Ranger District of the Los Padres National Forest. It doesn't appear that any of them had post offices, or even stores, but there is good off-road mine-site-hunting country in this region — in season, with permission.

In Los Angeles County, a grand pair of ghost camps exists high in the sky above Pasadena. Each had a post office in its day. One was called Echo Mountain, the other Mt. Lowe.

From the turn of the century until late in the 1930's a streetcar line

*LYTLE CREEK — For a short time there was noisy gold excitement deep in the San Bernardino Mountains, just north of Mt. Baldy at a site called Lytle Creek. This historic scene shows miners using hydraulic monitors to get at the gold-bearing gravels. Nearby, today, is an attractive Forest Service campground; little else.
—Photo from Security First National Bank.*

ran from downtown Los Angeles, through Pasadena and Altadena, up the sheer face of the granitic San Gabriel Mountains into the Angeles National Forest and ended at a station/pavilion in Rubio Canyon. From here an incredible incline railroad took people daily up the sheer mountain face to "the White City," Echo Mountain, directly over Altadena. There passengers got off the incline car and onto a small trolley that took them via dozens of curves and bends, even a complete loop, back to the site of a rustic but charming resort hideaway called Mt. Lowe. Several fires and a flood and then — what to call it, disinterest? — spelled the doom of the system. Today you can see both sites, but it requires some mountain driving, and some

hiking (check with the Forest Service about current road conditions). The trip is well worth it.

There are several ghost towns in Orange County. One of the more curious is the totally vanished Carbondale. And there is the old site of Silverado which is now pretty much off limits. The current town of Silverado, perhaps one of the most attractive sites in all of Southern California, sits near, but not smash-bang atop, the fabled old silver camp.

The Julian excitement is still marked by the mountain town of Julian which is very much like one of the Mother Lode communities. It was born out of the pull of the Mother Lode. Mike Julian, and the others

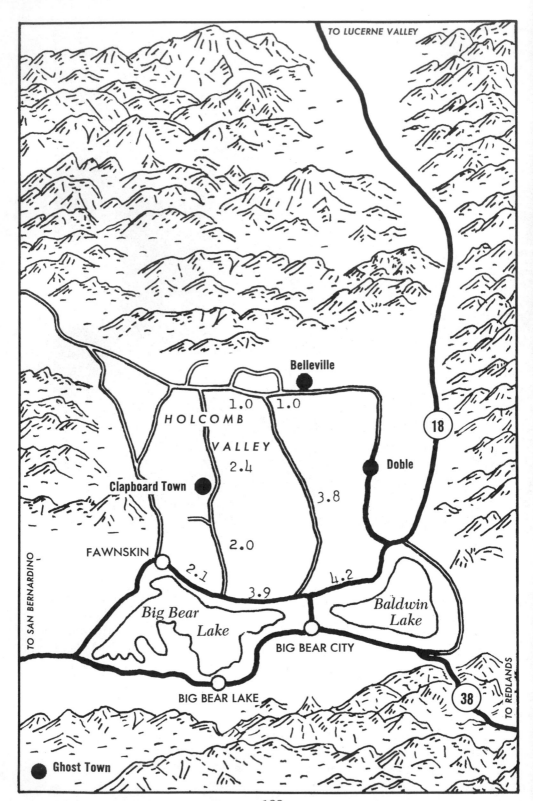

TO LUCERNE VALLEY

Belleville

1.0   1.0

HOLCOMB

VALLEY

2.4

Clapboard Town

3.8

Doble

18

2.0

FAWNSKIN

2.1

3.9

4.2

TO SAN BERNARDINO

Big Bear Lake

Baldwin Lake

BIG BEAR CITY

BIG BEAR LAKE

TO REDLANDS

38

Ghost Town

HOLCOMB VALLEY — While nothing much remains of the booming mining days of this gold area in the San Bernardino Mountains, this site, Holcomb Valley, is visited by hundreds of tourists each summer. Not far away is the giant Doble Mine where "Lucky" Baldwin mined for the precious yellow metal and added to his fortunes in Southern California.

who struck it rich here, had come to California to seek their fortunes in the Mother Lode and had drifted south.

The "son of Julian," if a camp could rightly and historically be called that, would be Cuyamaca, now adjacent to the Cleveland National Forest but in the Cuyamaca Rancho State Park, a large, rich, rewarding area for explorers. Just as Cerro Gordo helped finance an early Los Angeles, the Stonewall Jackson Mine at Cuyamaca helped San Diego become something more than a mission community.

There are many mines, mining camp sites, even a waystation or two in San Diego County. (Look for a lovely place called Lilac.) One of the "lost" ghost towns exists somewhere along the California/Baja California border, on the U.S. side. Somewhere here are the scars of a forgotten camp. All that is known about it is that "once a town was here." Yet to discover is exactley where and when, and even a name. A goodie to rank with Beveridge and Josephine...

Acknowledgements

For their support in helping me with writing, editing, revising, updating, correcting, redesigning and replanning this book I wish to thank the following:

Rick Anderson, Superintendent, Joshua Tree National Monument; Pat Brumm; Holly Bundock, Information Officer, National Park Service, Western Regional Office, San Francisco, California; Janet Buzzini, Assistant Public Information Officer, Shasta-Trinity National Forest, Redding, California.

Art Cowley, Public Affairs Officer, Sequoia National Forest, Porterville, California; William W. Escherick, director, Mapping Department, Automobile Club of Southern California; Ed Essertier, Public Information Officer, Department of the Interior, Washington D.C.; Karen Finlayson, Public Affairs Assistant, Eldorado National Forest, Placerville, California.

Patricia M. Flanagan, Information Specialist, Joshua Tree National Monument; Bob Grom, Biological Information Officer, Mammoth Ranger District, Inyo National Forest, Mammoth Lakes, California; Shirley Harding, Librarian, Death Valley National Monument; George A. Kenline, Forester, Big Bear Ranger District, San Bernardino National Forest, Fawnskin, California.

Kathy Moffitt, Forest Archaeologist, Sierra National Forest, Fresno, California; Larry Paynter, Public Information, California Department of Parks and Recreation, Sacramento, California; Don Porter, Information and Education Office, U.S. Forest Service (Retired), Newport Beach, California; Ed Rothfuss, Superintendent, Death Valley National Monument.

Jim Rothschild, Public Information Officer, Bureau of Land Management, Department of Interior, Sacramento, California; John Scull, Public Information Officer, California Desert District Office, Bureau of Land Management, Riverside, California; Linda Smith, Public Information Assistant, Stanislaus National Forest, Sonora, California; Zane G. Smith, Jr., Regional Forester, Pacific Southwest Region, U.S. Forest Service, Department of Agriculture, San Francisco, California.

Erwin Ward, Deputy Supervisor, Los Padres National Forest,

Santa Barbara, California; Jane Westenberger, Director of Information and Education, California Region, U.S. Forest Service, Department of Agriculture, San Francisco, California; Nord Whited, Recreation Staff, Regional Office, Pacific Southwest Region, U.S. Forest Service, Department of Agriculture, San Francisco, California.

As for the additional and new photographs in this book, credit goes to:

New photographs, this edition, by Russ Leadabrand; as well as from the collection of Russ Leadabrand; from the collection of Burton Frasher, Jr.; from the collection of Hank Johnston; from the Historical collection of the Security First National Bank; by Jim Rothschild.

And as for reference material consulted, I acknowledge:

Barbara Braasch, et al, *Gold Rush Country,*; E.I. Edwards author of *The Enduring Desert*; Walter N. Frickstad, compiler, author, *A Century of California Post Offices, 1848-1954*; Erwin G. Gudde, author of *California Place Names* and *California Ghost Camps* (with Elisabeth K. Gudde).

Mildred Brooke Hoover, Hero Eugene Rensch, Ethel Grace Rensch, authors of *Historic Spots in California* (with William N. Abeloe); Olaf P. Jenkins, et al, *Geologic Guidebook Along Highway 49 — Sierran Gold Belt — The Mother Lode Country*, prepared by the Division of Mines, State of California; Alice Goen Jones, editor of *Trinity County Historic Sites;* Remi Nadeau, author of *Ghost Towns and Mining Camps of California;* J.S. and R.J. Whiting, authors of *Forts of the State of California.*

And finally, and perhaps foremost, I thank Audrey Lazier Leadabrand, my wife, companion, severest critic and best editor, for her unflagging support, enthusiasm and participation.

Russ Leadabrand

"How It All Started: The Legend of 49" contributed by Sandy Clamage.

The Publisher